UP FOOL'S HILL
DOWN MEMORY LANE
ACROSS TIME

WHEELER POUNDS

Copyright 2018 © Bluewater Publications
Bluewater Publications
Killen, AL 35645
Bwpublications.com

First Edition

Library of Congress Control Number: 2018911180

Published in the United States by Bluewater Publications.

This work is based from the author's personal perspective.

Cover Illustration – Kate Gurganus at kategurganus.com
Interior Design - Maria Yasaka
Managing Editor – Angela Broyles

Books by Wheeler Pounds:

The Cherokee Hideaway BOOK ONE
ISBN 978-1-934610-64-0

The Cellar Vault BOOK TWO
ISBN 978-1-934610-79-4

The Spy Sanctuary BOOK THREE
ISBN 978-1-934610-24-4

CONTENTS

PREFACE

Grab a glass of iced tea, ease into your favorite chair and take a stroll with me down Memory Lane. We will travel through eighty years of life from an unfinished house at the end of a dirt road to destinations throughout the world. Get ready to climb Fool's Hill and descend to the valley below. As we travel, the scenery will be constantly changing until we can hardly remember how it looked when we began our hike.

I will be your guide as we travel through time, but you may in turn wish to organize your own hike as I am doing here. There are other paths that we would enjoy following which you could lead, but as of now, take a good sip of your beverage and let's begin.

As we journey through the eighty years of my life, there has been an almost complete transformation of our society from what I remember it to have been when I was young. In this trek, we will travel through life as I remember it as a young boy and continue to the present as it appears today. I discovered America on Sunday, September 25, 1938, in rural Fayette County, Alabama, so this is where we will begin our walk. It was in Fayette, Alabama, when I first became aware that I was beginning my life's journey, but I would soon move to an unfinished house in neighboring Walker County where I matured as an adult. I will point out certain significant things for you to be cognizant of as we pass through the years.

As we begin, I believe it necessary to caution you that we will have a steep hill to climb early in our journey. Fortunately we will start our ascent while we are young and full of energy, and this should be in our favor; but not always. The climb must be made while youth and inexperience tempt us to leave the proven path in order to explore life and this, too often, results in a loss of direction. On this journey we will follow the lighted path.

Let me give an explanation to you about the hill that we must climb. As a youngster, I picked up any job that I could get in order to make a little spending money. At that time we did not know the meaning of the word "allowance" and certainly did not receive one. I often worked for a nearby neighbor who needed help in clearing "new ground" in order to grow crops. It was a hot strenuous job: cutting bushes and removing rocks and roots from the field. On occasion, his wife would have pity on me and invite me to sit on the porch as we drank ice tea from quart jars. As I cooled off and drank my tea, she would take the opportunity to counsel me on certain things that she felt that every young boy should know. Often she would intersperse advice with the caution, "Now this is something that you should know in order to get over Fool's Hill."

According to her, everyone has the hill to climb, and we need to follow a detailed map that has been drawn to assist us as we climb. She informed me that the map to follow is the one drawn by the Creator after he made man. If that map is followed, it will give light in the darkness, and the way will be made clear. To some it becomes a difficult mountain to climb, while others find it to be a pleasurable ascent as they follow the map. After topping the hill, one must always be cautious lest he or she should stumble and fall on the descent, but the most difficult part has been traversed as age and experience clear many of the hurdles.

Be aware that we in our travels will climb the hill only once. Be prepared to stumble a few times, and maybe even fall, but it is important that we get right back up and continue to the top. This may require a longer climbing time to reach the crest, but the satisfaction of success will be worthy of the effort. Far too many surrender to the challenge, leave the path, and never reach the summit, thus a precious life is wasted. Foolish actions, habits, and harmful practices have consequences. After starting uphill there will be no turning around as the hill must be crossed. There will be no second chances to erase that which has been done and to be able to relive our life—what is done is permanent. One may have the opportunity to rectify regrettable mistakes, but the scars will remain; but never throw in the towel in defeat. With perseverance, the climb can be successful.

Fortunately, I have effectively climbed the hill, perhaps with the help of a caring neighbor and a quart of iced tea, and I am well on my way to the meadow below through which flows the River of Life. As your guide, I can describe the climb which must be made and implore one to be on the lookout for certain resting areas along the way which will provide a time to pause and take a second breath. There can be times to relax and reexamine the map and plot a safe course while the hike continues. Follow the guide as outlined in the Bible and consider the good examples set by those who have not strayed from the course, and the way will be made much easier. Take time to listen to the birds and smell the flowers that line the path. Be cautious as there will be thickets of briers and thorns if the path is not followed. Along the way there will be those who have erroneously considered that the use of pain killers, intoxicants, steroids, and other harmful drugs and habits will help them on the climb only to learn, many times too late, that they have destroyed their bodies. It should be easy to realize that people such as these do not set a good example for one to follow.

Travel with me as we climb Fool's Hill, stroll down Memory Lane, and cross eighty years of time.

CHAPTER ONE

CHANGES

I have made the trip up Fool's Hill and survived. I have been on the downward slope for some time now and am approaching the end of my allotted time to enjoy the blessings that have been afforded me through life itself. As I near the valley in which there are no exit paths, it is my intention to drain my memory vault so as to not carry all of its contents to my final resting place. There are so many who take those precious memories to their final resting place, and there is no greater loss than this. The elderly, one of our most valuable resources, are rich in memories and experiences of by-gone days, all of which are unique to the individual. When the coffin lid is closed for the final time, unless those memories have been shared and recorded, the valuable book which has taken a lifetime to write will be buried and lost forever. Cemeteries are filled with valuable irretrievable treasures.

Come along with me as I stroll through eighty years of memories. This book until now has been written without paper, and I wish to go an additional step and convert the unwritten to written, the unobtainable to obtainable, the unpreserved to the preserved. In no way can this be a glamorous story as it is not intended to be a novel, and should I insert glitz into this picture it would not depict the real me. Neither do I intend for this writing to portray an excellence in composition and grammar and sentence structure. I was never a star English student, and I would not want for one of my past English teachers who might read this to expect plagiarism. I will merely invite you to accompany me as I near the end of this journey, seeing that my hiking shoes are almost worn out and there will be no replacements. Enjoy the scenery as there will be sweeping changes.

I am fully aware as I write this that it reflects a very narrow perspective as it comes from the experience of a country boy whose childhood world was very small. City Slickers (no offense intended) who were reared in an entirely different environment, with paved streets and sidewalks, may find it difficult to walk along country paths and avoid the briars, poison oak, snakes, and stumbling stones along the way. Consider that one's perspective in life is formed from birth and is based on life experiences. Parents and their views and values are instilled in youngsters from the beginning of the child's life, and all will vary with different parentages. Peers also have a strong influence in child development. One must also figure in the time period that this growth occurred and individualism was molded. Such is what you will find in this reading. Like finger prints and snowflakes, no two personalities are identical. I feel fortunate to have been blessed with love, discipline, and guidance to insure an enjoyable life's journey. It has been one I feel worthy of sharing with others.

As a further introduction as to what you may expect as you read this writing, understand that my turn to live on this earth began in the year 1938, which means that I am three generations removed from the newcomers of today. The babies arriving today are welcomed into a vastly different world than the one in which I was born. The world in the thirties bears little resemblance to the present society, which is eighty years removed from the one I first knew. Whether or not this is advantageous or harmful for the children arriving now is open to debate, and I would not even venture a speculation. There are no apparent reasons to believe that with the passing of eighty more years the newborns of today will not look back and reflect on the vast changes which occurred during their lifetime. If the changes in that period of time are as extreme as that of my generation, and especially those of my parents and grandparents, future generations would be awed by a constantly changing, maybe even unrecognizable, world.

It was recently pointed out to me that the time I have been alive in the USA equals to about 1/3rd of the history of this country. This is computed by considering that from 1789 to 2018 totals 229 years or from 1776 to 2018 totals 242 years. With my eightieth year nearing, that would mean that I have witnessed approximately a third of this country's history. During this period there have been drastic changes in almost every aspect of life. As I contemplate these changes, I have concluded that documentation of them, as best I can recall, would leave a record for those who follow me. I want to drain my memory bank and deposit it here in this account of my life.

Every individual must choose the path that he or she will follow through life. As I reflect back on the path that I have selected, admittedly it was not crowded. Different paths lead to different destinations and through diverse terrain that presents assorted challenges, some leading to prosperity and happiness, others to poverty and heartbreak. I have been truly blessed while traveling the path that I have taken as it led me safely over Fool's Hill and down into a pleasant valley where I enjoy the food, flowers, animals, and crystal clear water which I share with a loving family. In this valley I have reserved a small plot as my final resting place, where I will be surrounded by family and friends who have also completed life's journey. I could ask for nothing better.

I could not expect my story to be typical of ones told by people who were reared in more harsh environments and who failed, by no fault of their own, to receive the parental supervision which would have led them to a more desirable path. That which is portrayed in this writing is seen through the lens of a country boy who received guidance over the stumbling stones and hurdles along the pathway. I was blessed with parents who showered me and my six siblings with abundant love. With this love came discipline. Spankings (switching's, not beatings) were doled out when needed, and with me they were effective. In today's world, paddling, switching, and spanking, are outlawed acts and rehabilitation has replaced punishment should one fail to adhere to the standards set by a lawful society. Is this good or bad? A child should never be subjected to a beating, but early childhood punishment, whether spankings or alternate methods, administered properly, is preferable to the need for rehabilitation after avoidable mistakes are made due to the lack of needed structure. I am not a fan of old quotes, but here I think one is appropriate. "An ounce of prevention is worth a pound of cure."

As we fast forward almost eighty years, it seems that the world in which I was born has evaporated as does the early morning fog. It is a much larger world today than the one which consisted of a lowly unfinished house, situated at the end of a dirt (often mud) road where I grew up. This realization is the impetus of this writing as I look back to my first remembrance, and attempt to compare it to the world of today. Changes are inevitable, but some are affected more by them than are others. From humble beginnings, any move upwards has a bearing on the quality of life an individual may experience. Using my journey through life as an example of the significance that change has impacted my trek throughout eighty years of time, I start my story at the beginning.

The world in which I was raised consisted of fifty-six acres of hilly terrain and plenty of trees to give a crosscut saw a good workout. This was not put to waste as my younger brother and I were introduced to the working ends of a crosscut as soon as we were able to use one. We rarely ever ventured far from this small world except to attend school, church services, and an occasional visit with relatives who did not live a long distance from our home. The longest distance that I recall traveling was on two or three forty mile trips to Birmingham and a school field trip to Florence, Alabama, until my senior year in high school when I traveled with the band to march and play in Montgomery at the inauguration of Big Jim Folsom as governor. It was on the return trip from Montgomery that I first entered a theatre, stopping in Birmingham at the Alabama Theatre to watch the movie *Twenty Thousand Leagues under the Sea*. As I viewed the bustling city with its tall buildings, I thought that was the ultimate, as big as it gets!

As the years passed my world began to expand, the fog began to lift, and a whole new world began to emerge. In 1965, my world had expanded to Japan where I camped at the foothills of Mt. Fuji. For the first two days, I was there the mountain was completely obscured by clouds and not visible. The camping was enjoyable, but it was difficult to accept that such a magnificent mountain loomed above us with none of it being exposed. On the third day, the clouds lifted and it was as though a new world had been created and a majestic mountain made to tower above us. The same scenario occurred on a trip to view and backpack the foothills of Mt. Denali in Alaska. The physical setting remained the same but a whole new panorama opened, and things appeared differently after the clouds lifted. This is the same world in which I was born, but the clouds have lifted and now I see an entirely different world which has expanded to the extent that now there seems to be no borders. When I return to the site of the small world in which I was reared, I hardly recognize it. The old house was torn down years ago. The well is capped and the fields where we grew food for the table are now pastures. The pine trees we planted as 4H projects were cut and made into paper many years ago. Fruit trees have stopped bearing and died sometime in the past, but the old black walnut and pecan trees that we planted have matured and still produce nuts. In the years following my exit from this primitive word to venture into Arkansas, where I started my life's education in the world outside of high school, I have explored more of this planet than I have ever thought possible.

When I first started traveling, I was too poor to buy a camera and film but eventually found a bargain on one in Japan, which I purchased. It did not take long, however, for me to realize that it is a cardinal sin to attempt to bore someone by showing travel pictures, so photography has never been one of my strong suits. Please excuse me if I yield to temptation and bore you by naming some of this big new world which I have been able to visit. If you want pictures, you will either need to find someone else who was there with a camera or go see the places for yourself. From the early home place to the present, my world has grown to include all fifty states, much of Canada from the east to the west, a brief excursion in Mexico, most European and many Asian nations: Scandinavia, England, Scotland, South America, the Holy Lands, Egypt, Turkey, Russia, Romania, Hungary Ukraine Brazil, Japan, Korea, journeys of Paul throughout Rome, Athens, Corinth, Ephesus, Crete, Rhodes, Patmos, islands in the Mediterranean, more principle world's cities than I could mention, and rivers such as the Rhine, Nile, and Danube that I have traveled. I have backpacked to the bottom of the Grand Canyon from both the north and south rims three times, rafted the Colorado river twice, visited and backpacked the majority of the Western and Southern National Parks, multiple times, including—see how fast this can get boring! Suffice it to say that there is a big world out there, and I have been blessed to have been able to enjoy the vast beauties created by God and also cities and structures built by man.

I even married a foreigner from Melrose Park, Illinois.

It is obvious that things are much different now than what I could ever imagine in my wildest dreams when I was young. Whether this is good or bad is subject to debate and might differ with each individual.

I speak only for myself and my lifetime observations as I intend to explore the changes that have occurred during my lifespan. Come along with me as I open my memory bank and sort through a variety of areas, which I will withdraw and record, first those that occurred when I was on the climb up Fool's Hill. I will recall memories from my formative years and I will then make a comparison as to what I see happening in today's world.

CHAPTER TWO

PATRIOTISM

Due to the fact that I hold a high regard for patriotism, I will make it my first category.

Then

When I was born in September 1938, Hitler had started making waves threatening world stability. I was born on a Sunday, and the week that had just ended was one of turmoil in Europe. Adolph Hitler had met with Neville Chamberlain and informed him that an attack on Czechoslovakia would take place unless Czechoslovakia was annexed to Germany. Although he first demanded that the area where the majority of the populations were German speaking people be annexed with a promise of no further hostilities to the region, it soon escalated into Hitler's conquest of the entire region, thus provoking the Second World War. One week after my birth on October 1, 1938 Hitler carried out his threat to invade Czechoslovakia, thus my first seven years of life saw the carnage which was created at the time of my birth. As a child, one of my first recollections was standing in our yard in Fayette, Alabama, where my father was preaching at the time and his attempt to point out some high flying airplanes, which I finally said that I saw but really didn't. This was surely the first lie I told him, and later I tried to not make a habit of it.

The year was around 1942 and the war was roaring in Europe and the Pacific. Rationing was in effect and times were hard for many families, including our own. We would soon move back to my mother's old home place in Walker County, Alabama, while my dad did his part in the war effort by guarding munitions at Anniston Ordinance Depot in Alabama. This left Mother with four children to care for, but she, as did countless others, accepted this as being necessary in order for our country and its allies to win a victory. At that time it seemed that everyone was on the same page—whip the Nazis and Japs and let us get back to enjoying the freedoms we inherited from the sacrifices made by our ancestors to create the greatest nation in history. Nobody was interested in learning to speak a new language.

The war came at a great price for every family that I knew. Though a very young child, I still remember the times when our family would receive wartime reports that another friend or relative had been killed or was missing in action. I could never forget the day Mother received the news that her brother-in-law, I.N. Sanford who was a navigator on a bomber flying out of England, was missing in action. He was never heard from again. A graduate of the University of Alabama, he had a young daughter born shortly before he left for combat. Jane never had the opportunity to get to know her father. Numerous accounts of such losses can be told and retold, but such was the great price that was paid so that we are now able to enjoy the greatness of this nation. The First World War had already been fought and a great price paid for it. I still saw the scars from it in that a great uncle, Dewey Pounds, had been a victim of a chemical gas attack which caused permanent brain damage leaving him incapable of carrying on an intelligent conversation. He carried this burden from a very young age until his death, never being able to live a meaningful and productive life. This too was the price paid for our freedom.

The war years were an era when patriotism was not questioned. This threat to our country and freedoms was met by those who were willing to sacrifice their lives so that our enemies would be crushed. The military draft was in effect, but many volunteered to meet the challenge and went off to war, many to never return. The entire nation celebrated when victory was won and life could resume with the threat being eliminated, but the war was won at a great price for almost every family I knew.

I entered school when the war was nearing its end, and there was no doubt that patriotism was at its height. In school, each day would begin with a pledge of allegiance to the flag, which would be recited with our hand over our hearts while facing the flag. Some teachers would also follow the pledge with a Bible reading and the Lord's Prayer. Sporting events would call on the preachers of the different denominations in the town to lead a prayer for the safety of the players after the playing of the National Anthem, where everyone stood and the men removed their hats. The nation as a whole took pride in our country and the principles upon which it was founded.

Now

Almost eighty years have passed and times have changed; some say that it is for the better while others declare that everything has gone to pot. It would be hard to deny that we live in a different world today. The generation preceding me and my generation have probably lived in the most exciting period, with the greatest changes, of any generation in history. As I look around at the world today, I sometimes attempt to imagine what the reaction of the people who preceded me by eighty years would be should they be able to return to see the world as it has evolved following their deaths. At that time, divided patriotism resulted in the Civil War and following that the South was struggling to recover from the defeat.

There have been many changes and advancements since the surrender of the Confederate army and the patriotic Southern soldiers went home in defeat. With the many changes since that time, I wish to explore the inner-self of what men have become in regard to their willingness to lay down their lives for a cause in which they believe. It is the question of how have the drastic changes in life styles affected the present generation. Are we still the patriotic people who would once again heed the call to arms should our freedoms be threatened once again? Would we stand as one people and rise up and fight to insure our sovereignty as a nation? Would we be as eager as those of the generation that preceded me to rise up to take up arms and fight in our defense? If required, where will these soldiers come from? We should all say a prayer that it will never be necessary to have these questions answered.

The strength and power of the United States is presently a deterrent for any lesser power to seriously contemplate aggression against us, although there are terrorist groups who are continually plotting to find ways to create as much havoc as possible. We have been lulled into a sense of complacency and security with few outside the military giving much thought to a strong defense of our country.

On the positive side one might question whether it would be necessary to pour troops into battle as in previous wars. The advancements in military technology and equipment will certainly alleviate some of the need for ground troops, but will these modernizations be enough to successfully fight a war? In an attempt to explore this question regarding the status of our military in regard to what will be the need should another world war erupt, the advancements in military weaponry, aircraft, drones, missiles, heavy weapons, and advanced tactics would surely go a long way in successfully fighting a war without putting troops on the ground, but there will always be a need for the Army, Navy, Air Force, Marines, and Coast Guard. At the present it appears that this need can be met by those who enlist to offer their service to this country but there is relative peace in the world now. Should there be conflicts in the future such as the one in which I was born, would there be ample patriotism in this country to rise up to the challenge? I would like to believe that the need would be met, but there are alarming signs that more and more of our military age young men (and now women) display a blatant disrespect for the flag, pledge, anthem, prayer, and country. Failure to salute (some even burn) the flag, to stand when the National Anthem is played and such examples of disrespect are alarming to me.

Pray for peace in this world!

CHAPTER THREE

RELIGION

Then

One of the foundations upon which our country was founded was religious freedom. The belief in God was so strong among our forefathers that it was even inscribed on our money. The founding fathers were fervent in their beliefs. This fervor was shown in the extensive acceptance of religion. Some such as the Quakers and Shakers got only limited participation, yet their beliefs and practices were accepted as were all others. There were also new religious bodies which were formed here, and they too were accepted, the Mormons (Church of Jesus Christ of Latter Day Saints) being an example. Many religious denominations had their beginnings in the countries from which the immigrants to this country had left and their establishment here was a springboard on which the spread of religion swept the new country. Religious tolerance was practiced and every citizen was free to accept their chosen denomination.

Not only was religion accepted but religious services were well attended. Devotion to Christianity was instilled in the very fabric of family life. During that era there was not so much emphasis placed on material things, which were then in short supply in many cases. Hell fire and damnation preachers were effective in convincing people that they needed to turn or burn. "Life may be hard here on earth, but a better place was waiting for the faithful," was their emphasis in sermons. Creek banks on Sunday afternoon were often crowded by those attending baptismal ceremonies. Revivals (often referred to as Protracted Meetings or Gospel Meetings) often lasted two weeks, and in many of the small church buildings the summer's heat was almost unbearable in the small crowded buildings, yet there would be an overflow crowd almost every night with people sitting on the raised pulpit and in the windows. Some preferred that to the hard wooden homemade board benches provided for seating. Local funeral homes, businesses, and even politicians provided hand held fans which some of the plus size ladies, and others, utilized to the fullest. The ladies wore their "Sunday go to meeting" clothes (always dresses, never pants) and hats (some quite large), but many of the men were comfortable in their freshly washed overalls. With many children, shoes were optional but those who had them, many times a few sizes too large, wore them proudly.

With some preachers, the sermon would last about two hours at which time the toddlers would start to get restless and the older children would whisper among themselves having no idea what the preacher had been saying for the last hour or two. The Holy Scriptures were the furthest thing from their minds, and it would be difficult to find one who could even tell what the topic of the sermon was about. Mother had her own way of keeping us kids in line during church services. She would make us kids sit in front of her, and if we started to misbehave she would thump our ears. Occasionally, when an alert preacher would see that he was about to lose his audience, he would slap the podium and raise his voice to a shout to wake everyone up who was on the verge of dozing off. There were a lot of scriptures quoted (not necessarily read) with book, chapter and verse included. Sin was strongly condemned, with the admonition that unless people failed to purge it from their lives they would go straight to hell when they died.

Young people welcomed the occasion to look over the opposite sex and check out the available crop of potential spouses. After a budding prospect was sighted, the long walk home was sometimes made hand in hand with a willing "date." It was by this method that many friendships resulted in marriage. On a personal note, my parents met at a Gospel Meeting, but this may not be as it might first appear. Mother went to the services to hear the preacher, and Daddy went to play marbles with the boys outside and to look over the crop of females when they exited the building. Mother caught Dad's eye, maybe vice-versa, or perhaps it was mutual, but it did not take long for them to get back in touch with the preacher to have him perform their marriage ceremony. Mother immediately set in to instill in him a little Bible knowledge, as it has been told that he was never inside a church building before they met. Her effort was so effective that he spent the remainder of his life preaching the Word.

Preachers boarded with church members for the duration of the protracted meeting and were sometimes paid for their services in farm goods as there was very little money available to pay them. One payoff was that the good cooks of the congregation signed up to feed the preacher, and it was then that the old rooster would meet its fate and end it all in a frying pan. In addition, there might be pork or beef from the smoke house where the meat was preserved. There was always a big kitchen table filled with fresh vegetables and fruit prepared as only a country cook could deliver. A dessert of fresh peach or blackberry cobbler, apple pie or other desserts followed the vegetable feast. For drinks, cold well water, sweet milk or buttermilk, and sometime tea were offered. Ice was a rare commodity and drinks were rarely served colder than the water drawn from the well. Milk was often placed in lidded gallon jugs, then placed in buckets which were let down by ropes into the cold well water. A good revival where there were a lot of baptisms was payoff enough as the preacher was there to save souls and not to become prosperous. The Lord would provide!

Many churches provided toilets which were often needed after the long trip by foot, horseback, or wagons or after (sometimes during) a long sermon. They were usually placed behind the church building with the men's on one side and ladies' on the other. It was not uncommon for there to be a lot of coming and going, especially with the younger crowd, during the services. The toilets were getting a workout although many times it was probably not as great a case of urgency as the departing person would want you to believe.

Small stands were placed on the walls of the church buildings where kerosene lamps were placed for lighting. After a period of time, the ceilings above the lamps would be blackened by smoke. In the wintertime, there were those who had the assignment to arrive at the church building early enough to build a fire in the potbellied stove which was normally located in the front middle of the building. There was usually a coal pile conveniently located outside. A coal scuttle and poker were usually stored in a corner along with the straw broom, various printed items, many times in disarray, and a box of dust rags torn from an old sheet.

Many of the country churches had cemeteries where families buried their dead. A chosen Sunday during the year was assigned to have a homecoming and decoration. This would provide the occasion for the social event of the year. Relatives would gather for a dinner on the grounds and an afternoon singing. A long outdoor wooden table was usually constructed to hold the mounds of covered dishes which cooks would present as their offering to the cause. There was always more than enough to feed all comers. Aunts, uncles, cousins and other friends and relatives would utilize this time to get to know one another better and catch up on the happenings since their last meeting. While the adults would stand around and reminisce, the youngsters would be involved in playful activities. For Sunday services, the building would be packed as was the afternoon singing. It was commonplace for all extra available chairs to be set out in advance in anticipation of the crowd that would attend. The best singers from all over would never miss a good singing.

Vendors jumped at the opportunities to set up where there would be a lot of people congregated. Many knew or had recorded when and where each decoration would draw the greatest number, and they would go on Saturday and set up to be prepared to do business as people came to decorate graves and attend the Sunday services and festivities. Common vendor items consisted of crushed flavored ice cones, ice cream packed in small lidded cups (a small flat spoon was provided), popsicles, and ice cream bars which were kept cold by a chest type freezer that was kept in the truck, plugged in, and kept cold until time to go and sell the goods. Other vendors peddled all different types of trinkets. It was also common to have Bible salesmen there peddling their King James Version of the Bible. The Dixon Bible was one of the most expensive, yet one of the best sellers. It was a favorite among many of the preachers and came highly recommended, much to the delight of their salesmen.

Cemeteries would be cleaned and decorated for the homecoming. Most graves at that time had dirt raked up to a point over the body and they would undergo a fresh raking, and fresh cut flowers would be placed along the top. Much pride was taken in growing the best flowers and making the nicest arrangements that would adorn the grave of the loved one. After the flowers dried, they would be removed and properly disposed of. Young children were taught to respect graves, and that they should never be walked on or desecrated in any way.

Sometimes on occasions there were efforts to establish a church in a community when there would be no building available in which to meet. The answer to that was to build a brush arbor under which the meeting would take place. This was an effective approach as people would attend for curiosity's sake. There were occasions when a tent would take the place of a brush arbor. Many times these meetings would result in enough conversions that would enable there to be a congregation established and a building constructed.

Preachers did not hesitate to call sin, "sin", and warn of its consequences by describing a fiery hell waiting for those who did not accept Christ. This would be followed by portraying a home where there would be eternal bliss. There was always a plea that the sinners forsake their evil ways and get right with the Lord. At the end of a sermon, there was a plea that one respond to the will of God and be saved from sins. Most country congregations had their favorite river, creek, or pond where baptisms were performed. Sometimes during a protracted revival meeting there would be a number of individuals who would respond to the invitation plea and were then ready for baptism that would wash away their sins. The people of the congregation would gather at the banks of the baptismal hole and sing songs: "O happy Day" being a favorite as the preacher led the converts into the water for their immersion. As they emerged from the water they were embraced, wet clothes and all, by the congregants who welcomed them into the fold. After a prayer thanking God for the power of his Word which moved the new converts to obedience and a plea that they have a long and faithful life in his service, the crowd dispersed with shouts of joy.

While growing up, our family was taught to respect others and behave as a Christian should behave. We were always taken, not sent, to church services whenever the church doors were opened. Sundays were to be considered the Lord's Day and that excluded fishing and other recreational activities on that day. Wednesday nights were also reserved for Bible study. A prayer of blessing was always offered before each meal. Eyes were expected to be closed during a prayer.

Such are my recollections of religion when I was young.

Now

Yes, the things described above were all taken from my personal memory bank-vendors, brush arbors, tents, grave diggings, and all. Things have changed drastically in these eighty years. There now is an assault on religion, and the teaching of God and Christ are ridiculed and in many places banned, including our public education institutions. The teachers who began a class period with a Bible reading and prayer when I was young would be without a job if they attempted to do the same today. In a greater part of our public institutions of higher education today the majority of those who are teaching our young are declared atheists and ridicule anyone who is a believer. The Bible is declared to be a book not worthy of serious study. The principles taught in the Bible are to be ignored as one should feel free to live their life as they see fit in a way which would give them the most personal satisfaction. Anyone who believes that there is a heaven and hell as is taught in the Bible is a victim of brain washing by unfit parents. Such parents should be required to enroll in parenting classes where they could be taught the proper way to raise their young free from such restrictions which the Bible and Church places on them. There are no sexual sins, but any lifestyle should be accepted and participation is encouraged.

When I was young, maintaining the purity of one's body and refraining from unhealthy habits were encouraged and emphasized. Family values with close and loving relationships were considered to be the glue that helped to make this country great. "The family that prays together stays together," was a frequent quote. The golden rule was taught and practiced. Respect for authority, with God being the highest, was taught to the very young so as to insure compliance throughout life. Laws were made to be obeyed and penalties were to be expected for breaking them. The elderly were elevated as a source of learning through their experiences of a lifetime, and they were respectfully treated and spoken to. Christians were all considered to be members of God's family and were often addressed as brother and sister.

Large sums of money are now spent to make many "mega" church buildings as beautiful and comfortable as a budget will allow after paying the pulpit minister, associate minister, youth minister, sports director, mission minister, minister of music, van drivers, secretaries, custodian, maintenance and grounds keepers the large salaries they demand.

These buildings contain a lot of expensive cut glass windows, along with vast open spaces inside that only serve to make use of the elaborate air conditioning and heating systems which are required to provide the best comfort possible. Then there are the elaborate sound systems vital to getting the speaker's voice out of the rafters, chandeliers and lighting necessary to penetrate the vast interior. There are decorative exterior columns, arches, steeples, groomed landscape, paved and lined parking spaces, carpeted floors and padded pews. In the eighty years of my life, church buildings have come a long way from the brush arbors with dirt floors.

There is one problem, however. On any given Sunday, many of the buildings that are constructed to hold a thousand people could accommodate a Greyhound bus (almost another relic of the past) load of people and still have plenty of empty pews that would comfortably seat any new comers. Those that are there have little idea of who the people are who habitually sit on the other side of the building. The family aspect of Christian families meeting together has virtually disappeared. The sermons are watered down to the point that the preacher tells the congregants what they want to hear regardless of what the Bible teaches regarding the topic. After all, the preacher has a high paying job that he must protect and cannot afford to be stepping on the toes of some of the best contributors. Very little Bible is quoted or read except for an occasional text being used, and sin is no longer condemned. I am aware that I am painting everything with a broad brush, but I believe that one must concede that today we have more of a social gospel than a Biblical one. Entertainment has replaced heartfelt religion in many cases as the sport complex attached to the sanctuary is often times more in use and better attended than the worship services. Bands and singing groups are often advertised in an effort to boost attendance. It is uncommon now to hear young preachers quote book, chapter and verse from the Bible as I remember them doing from my childhood. There are exceptions of course, and I hope that I can be proven wrong on this issue.

The long, wooden outdoor tables have been replaced by swanky air conditioned fellowship halls and KFC does the rooster killing and cooking. Marbles are no longer shot on the outsides grounds but in many church buildings a state of the arts gym offers a place to play almost any indoor sport. If transportation is needed, a church bus or van will give one a ride. A long walk to and from church services would surely have an adverse effect on attendance in today's age.

The plight of small country churches is very different. Many have closed their doors and the buildings torn down, sit empty, or have been converted into community halls or shops. With others, their cemeteries are the threads that keep their doors open. There are small groups who have never attended regular church services anywhere except the home church in which they were raised, with attached cemeteries in which the family has been buried for generations. These will continue in attendance until the last member joins the others in the cemetery, after which the doors will be locked on the building to be opened only when the young return yearly for the homecoming and decoration. With many of the surviving congregations the young have moved away and only the elderly are left to carry on. Unless a revival of interest can be restored in these congregations and there be those young enough to replace the elderly members, it will be only a matter of time before their doors are locked except for that special Sunday of each year when family shall return to decorate the graves and honor the dead who once made the place a vibrant place to assemble and worship God. For one Sunday each year the walls may ring again with singing and perhaps a sermon preached. Those in attendance will socialize and leave declaring what a great day it has been. The artificial flowers will then be left to fade and some blown away by the wind, many times almost forgotten until next year's calendar reminds them that it is time to do it again. How long and how many cycles and generations this will continue until forest and weed rule the area is an unknown. One thing is certain, if the next eighty year follows the example of the past eighty, it might not be forest and weeds which will replace the beloved cemetery but roads, buildings, or industries that will occupy that treasured land. In the past eighty years, strip mining has also been a culprit leaving vast areas unrecognizable. Many also wonder if religion itself as we know it will be recognizable. If the trend continues that relegates religion as being for those ignorant enough to take an old outdated book and make it a center of their lives, and a stand is not made in its defense, there might be a landscape of deserted church buildings, or maybe those turned into historical museums so that the populous can see what once was.

Sermons today are preached to appease the audience and sin is no longer called sin, nor is it condemned in many pulpits. The idea that there is a devil has largely been ignored and the word "hell" is only used in profanity. People are no longer responsible for their actions, and a lot of fault is placed on extenuating circumstances, whatever that might be. Religion has become more of a social organization where the teaching of the Bible has been relegated to the status of an unimportant book destined to remain unopened on the shelf where it has become covered with dust.

Worship services themselves have undergone a significant change. Worshipers now expect to meet in complete comfort with thermo-stat-controlled temperature, adequate lighting, and cushioned pews. Gone now are the kerosene lamps, hand and wall fans, and hard home-made wooden benches. I remember when prayer was led in church services, the leader of the prayer would kneel on one knee, every head bowed and all eyes closed—not so anymore. Bibles were opened and references were checked. Now when I look around during services I see not books but the Bible displayed on electronic screens. With a few taps of the fingers additional verses appear and there is no turning of pages.

Sound amplifiers enable the speaker to be heard and there are individual amplifiers provided for the hearing impaired in many buildings. The messages are taped in larger congregations for future use and some are broadcast live or recorded on radio or television. During the passing of years new gospel songs have been written, and the younger song leaders tend to want to sing those which have been written more recently. Now "Rock of Ages" and "The Old Rugged Cross" have been replaced with songs such as "As a Deer Pants for the Water" and "These Are the Days of Elijah". Song books have become largely unused as the songs selected are projected on a large screen that all can see. I prefer the old songs and never tire when singing them, but I must admit that the projected words and music are more convenient than having to turn pages in a song book. Contemporary gospel music is also big with some as are gospel quartets and singing groups. Most of this has evolved over the past eighty years.

The methods of donations given to the church are even making a change. When I was young, my mother would put a coin, usually a nickel or dime, in the hands of each of her six children to place in the collection plate. She wanted us to become accustomed to placing money in the plate as it passed. That does not seem like much money now, but then after Dad made his contribution it was almost like the poor widow throwing in her two mites. Then almost all contributions to the church were made in cash. Now the preferred method of giving is by check and now plastic. Many of the church leaders now prefer the card method because the donor does not have to be in attendance to give when the collection plate is passed. Bank accounts can be set up to automatically deduct the contributions each week or month and one does not have to bother getting out of bed on Sunday mornings to go to religious services to pay for salvation.

In our family, Sunday was always a day which was to be the Lord's day. We did no work on Sundays nor did we fish or participate in sports. Wednesday nights were also reserved for Bible study. Back then the stores did not open on Sundays and "Blue Laws" were passed barring them from doing so. Many considered it to be a day of rest after a hard week of labor. Today anything goes on Sundays. Stores and restaurants are wide open for business (except a few like Hobby Lobby and Chick-Fil-A), and some like gas stations and Wal-Mart are open 24-7.

Will some never get over Fool's Hill? We read that it is the fool that has said in his heart that there is no God. His creation and presence can be seen in his blessings and handy work which we daily enjoy. Will the stand be made by the faithful? Eighty years from now I will not be around to know the answers to these questions, nor will you, but I pray that the news will be good and that faith in God and his promises will endure the test of time.

CHAPTER FOUR

EDUCATION

Then

To give my perspective on the whole of public education in my lifetime, I must start in the fall of 1944 when I entered the first grade in a small coal mining and railroad town. A nice brick school building in Parrish replaced the one room school house in the mining town nearby where my mother had entered the first grade. When a person turned six years old before October 1st of a given year, it was time to go to school. If I had been born six days later I could not have entered school the year that I did, so I was one of the youngest first graders in school. No preschool programs were available, so the first grade was the starting point in "grade school" as it was then called. My mother, born in 1914, would tell of walking the two or three miles to the Big Ridge schoolhouse as transportation was not then provided. My father, also born in 1914, lost his mother at preschool age (around five years old). His father then joined the ranks of the hobos and caught a train, or trains, that ended up in Texas where he stayed for a period of time. In 1920 there was no governmental structure in place to provide adequate placement of homeless children so Dad was left at a very young age to fend for himself. Dad was the youngest of three boys and they were left to be cared for by an older sister who had married young. As school attendance was not enforced, their childhood public education was very limited. When very young, Dad took off to live and survive in the local forest and on the rivers where he received his vocational education. There were a few families who lived on the river banks or in the forest who befriended him and allowed him to stay with or near them, and they received work from him in exchange for their generosity. One family in Arley in Winston County can still show people a rock shelter located on their land under which Dad built a pole wall for escape from the elements and where he would spend much of the winter hunting and trapping. Ninety years later some of the poles still remain where he left them. This account is given to show that at that time education did not always come from a structured class environment. Some received their education in classrooms; there were others whose school desks remained unoccupied the majority of time and were relinquished to others after three or four years. Illiteracy was commonplace at that time and many more had very limited abilities to do basic reading and writing. Education has made great strides since that time.

First grade teachers focused on reducing the illiteracy rate by teaching the basics. The three R's were named as being essential, although the ones who coined that phrase apparently needed to have spent a little longer in the classroom themselves to get the correct spellings: reading, riteing, (writing) and rithmetic, (arithmetic). Textbooks and the chalk board were used to assist in these efforts. Recess was my favorite period of the day, as I never really took a liking to remaining silent and paying attention to what the teacher was trying to get me to learn. My wandering mind never seemed to quite settle down when I was a captive audience. Perhaps this is an area in which childhood is the same now as then and which will be eighty years from now despite all the pills that can be prescribed.

Reading

Then

Words are the foundation of this category comprised of letters of the alphabet. One of the first things a first grade teacher did was to require the student to know and recite the alphabet. Some students entered the first grade having had it taught while others had no skills in school work. Many children suffered academically because their parents had very little schooling and were unable to teach them the basics needed to excel in their grades. Children with parents who could only sign their names with an X, which many did, were at a decisive disadvantage in their early school years. It was difficult for the children of these parents to rise to greater heights, and it was the duty of a good teacher to help them do so. Fortunately, there were many dedicated teachers who inspired a number of students to seek loftier goals and live fruitful lives.

Reading was a necessary start for the young students to meet the requirements of a sound education. Learning the alphabet was the starting point, but it was not enough. In order for a letter to have a meaningful life, it must find a partner, or partners, to construct a meaningful word. In order for the word to come alive, it too must find a partner, or partners to form a sentence which then looks for partners which will then constitute a paragraph. When all this has had an organizational assembly and the paragraphs join forces the results can take readers from the classroom to anywhere the joined words will take them.

The teacher would take chalk in hand and begin teaching the young student words that had only found three or four letters as partners; (ant-bat-cat-dog-eat;), and so the words would appear on the black board. The word would be pronounced a number of times as it appeared on the blackboard. The standard practice for my teacher was for her (always female in elementary school for me) to have us copy the word as she had written it on the black board into our ruled tablets to be used for home work. It was in this manner that I was first introduced to Dick, Jane, their dog Spot, and others. I surmise that Dick and Jane met a lot of first graders as they appeared in classrooms long before, and after, my first grade year.

It was always hard for me to justify the homework requirement as I had so many chores to do before darkness fell. The first few years that I was in school all studying (which was minimal) had to be done by light from a "coal oil" or kerosene lamp as electrical lines had not yet reached the remote section of the state where we lived. Needless to say, homework often came up short.

Reading gradually carved out a special place in my life. Due to very limited pre-school preparation, it took a while for me to get the hang of converting words into pictures. When I finally caught on, the story of Helen Keller at the well when the word "water" realistically entered her vocabulary had meaning and added significance to my efforts to read. I can vividly recall when only the pictures in a book made any sense, and the printed word was like we would later say about things we could not understand, "That's Greek to me." I then took to words "like a duck takes to water" to use another cliché (Cliché? Where did that word come from with an apostrophe stuck over the e? I see that I still have a lot to learn about words).

After learning to read and finding out that words could give me an escape from our little house at the end of the road, I read practically everything I could get my hands on. The first book that I remember reading was "Black Beauty". Being an animal lover, "Black Beauty" took me on such an enjoyable ride that I wanted other books to take me to places where I could never otherwise go. Later in high school I read the majority of the books available in the library. Admittedly, the little library was stuck under the stairs that led to the second floor and had very little space. Therefore, the selections of subjects were very limited. There were books available however that would take the reader through the Amazon Rain Forest and a ride down the wild river, and others would allow a safari through the plains of Africa or a trek to Lapland, the land of the reindeer. In my mind these stories are timeless, relevant eighty years ago and will still be relevant eighty years from now. Sadly, it appears that electronics are swiftly replacing printed material. Never in my wildest dreams would I have thought that one day those words would take wheels and wings and carry me to every state in the USA, or that I would travel above the Arctic Circle in Norway near Lapland and later near the Arctic Circle in Russia. I have traveled to Brazil, land of the Amazon River and Forest and experienced some of what my childhood imagination could only contrive. I saw pictures and read of Mt Fuji, and now I have been able to climb to its top. In the Bible I read of Moses and his basket of bulrushes in the Nile River, and now I have had the opportunity to have spent seven days on the river of which I had previously formed only mental pictures developed from words. I could continue in this vein relating voyages on the Rhine in Germany or long excursions along the banks of the "Blue Danube," as words picture it. I have put real pictures to those imaginary ones of Biblical places such as the whole of the Holy Lands (three trips): Rome, Athens, Corinth, Ephesus, Patmos, Rhodes, Crete, and I have taken pictures of places in almost all of the European countries, Scandinavia, England, Scotland, Ukraine, Romania, Hungary, and Canada. I will stop here because I have already acknowledged the fault of many travelers to want to show too many pictures to an unwilling audience. Suffice it to say that in my childhood my photo albums were filled with word generated pictures, and today my albums are filled with the actual pictures from which the imaginary ones were created by my readings. The ones from my own camera that are missing are wild Safari treks in Africa as this has never been my destination. I'm holding on to those that I still have stored in imaginary albums as I have no plans to replace them with actual ones.

I could not have imagined that the scenes formed by those words that I read as a young boy would materialize into fully developed pictures captured on film by my own camera. Words are more than letters of the alphabet placed in an organized printed form but are pictures of every fantasy; the more skilled the writer, the clearer the emerging picture. I owe this treasure to my first teachers whom I now consider to be word photographers and who had the patience to instill in me a love of reading.

I can never forget how much I looked forward to getting the *Weekly Reader* which always contained subjects of interest. There were also the *Grit* newspapers which were sent to our house to be sold by my brother. I would always read one before folding it back into its original condition to be read again by the buyer. Reading about current events made the dead end road that led away from our house stretch a little farther into the outside world.

Now

Words are still words and pictures are still painted, but the changing times have basically removed them from the hard cover of a book to an electronic screen where they can be read. If you want a picture of the place the words are carrying you, your imagination no longer has to come into play. Simply bring up Google, tell it the words that interest you, and you will be able to travel to the site of interest. This relegates the imagination to take the back seat, but one must admit that it delivers far greater accuracy than the imagination ever could. However there is a hitch here. The present generation has become so accustomed to having electronics showing them pictures of everything through computers, televisions, movies, and video cameras, that words are becoming obsolete except in conversations. Why take the effort to sit down and read when it can be watched with little effort?

Who can predict where this may lead in another eighty years? Will books and printed words as we now know them become obsolete? I would not have the courage to even venture a guess.

Writing

Then

The confession that I have retired my old ink pen and am now writing this by punching letters on a key board is enough testimony to the fact that times have changed since I sat in a small desk in elementary school. I well remember the time that the writing instrument of choice was the yellow lead pencil. All classrooms had a pencil sharpener affixed to a wall, and it bore its share of use during the day. Boys thought it to be an honor when the teacher would choose one to empty the shavings of sharpened pencils. Dusting erasers fit in the same category. It was something to boast about to parents when they got home. "I emptied the pencil sharpener today," was an announcement that was always made with an expanded chest.

If ink was used, it came in a small jar separate from the ink pen. To fill the pen the point was inserted just below the level of the ink and a small lever on the side drew the ink into a bladder inside the pen. The writing point had a split in the middle which allowed the ink to flow evenly on the paper. When the ball point pen made its appearance on the market, it made as much excitement to me as did the appearance of the chain saw that took the place of a crosscut. Neither was cheap when they first hit the market but well worth the price if one could afford to buy them.

Here I must confess that my handwriting leaves plenty to be desired. I take comfort in the fact that it is generally legible but I, following the trend, do not write cursive as often as I once did. My early teachers required a printing tablet where the letters were printed with a line underneath for the student to imitate while copying. Both capital and lower case letters were studied. Later words were given to be copied, many times as homework.

Now

In some schools it is reported that the teaching of cursive is almost a thing of the past. Keyboards have taken the place of writing pads, and texting has made its own life with its abbreviated means of spelling. The reader may get a broader view of this by answering the following question; how many handwritten letters or cards have you received through the mail in the past year? At one time this was the way of choice to communicate with friends, relatives, business, etc. Verbal communications and short e-mails have virtually replaced mailed letters. Junk mail has replaced personal mail, which the majority of recipients chunk in the trash can without taking the time to open and read.

Arithmetic

Then

It was here that the blackboard came into full play. It was also here that my constant fear was that the teacher would call me to the front of the room to complete a numbers (doing numbers was what my parents called arithmetic) problem. Getting past simple addition was plenty enough challenging for me, multiplication pushed my limits, and algebra completely pushed me off the deep end. My dad was given multiplication charts for all the children in the family from an insurance salesman, and it was from this that I learned the multiplication tables. Arithmetic teachers expected that additions, subtractions, and multiplication tables be learned by rote memory, and you would be invited to the front of the room to share that memory with your fellow classmates. Learning this and being able to say them was a great incentive to avoid embarrassment before those classmates. Teachers always kept little tricks up their sleeves to nudge reluctant students to try a little harder.

Whereas I was always anxious for reading class period to arrive, not so much so did I embrace arithmetic. In keeping with my likes and dislike, I will be brief in my comments regarding arithmetic because frankly, I do not know enough to write about it.

Now

I have been very lax in my eighty years to learn much more about arithmetic than I knew eighty years ago. I managed, through a lot of study to pass the basic math courses required in college, but I did not sign up for any further studies. I know that now I must refer to the subject as math instead of numbers or arithmetic, but I will not venture beyond this to attempt a knowledgeable analysis of changes. I do remember that the slide rule was frequently used in my younger years, but calculators have sent them packing as they have done in many aspects of math. Addition, subtraction, multiplication and division are now all done electronically.

Education as a whole has made drastic changes over the years. Preschool programs offer a child a head start in achieving a sound education. Today there are many more mothers in the workplace outside the home than when I was young, and children are left in daycares where their teaching begins at an early age, giving them an advantage over the child who enters school without the early training. Children reared by a single, uneducated parent and from a low income, minimally- supervised family, are sometimes unable to speak, write, or even understand English. These children already have a strike against them when they enter school. Money is spent to modernize school buildings, but in many cases grades do not improve. Teachers today are inundated with volumes of paper work that has little to do with educating a child. Some teachers are required to spend more time maintaining order in a classroom than in teaching the subject of the lesson. Things have truly changed in this aspect of education. When I was a student in elementary and high school, the big problems facing teachers were students who talked as the lesson was presented, chewed gum, shot spitballs using a rubber band or threw wads of paper. Teachers were always treated with respect even though they might not have reached the height of adoration with some students as they did with others. This sometimes is not true today, and in some cases teachers suffer abuse at the hands of a student who is a constant problem maker and has no desire to be in the classroom. Too often this disrespect and abuse are allowed to go unpunished and the disruptive child is allowed to cause daily problems interfering with the education of those who want to receive an education. Any time spent by a teacher in an effort to maintain discipline in the classroom is time stolen from the endeavors of the conscientious teacher whose goal is to give the student a quality education. Continued disruptions in the classroom that interfere with the ability of a teacher to teach and a student to learn should be addressed immediately by the administration and remedied immediately by the most effective way possible. It is the good administrator who can maintain discipline within the school and has procedures established which will be effective as different scenarios arrive and must be addressed. The teachers and administration, with maybe security officers in the mix, all working together must maintain order at all times. Good teachers must be rewarded, and the few who are incompetent should not be permitted to stay in the classroom and rob a child of one important year of education. The formative years in a child's education are more important than providing one person a salary that is not justified. The whole classroom of students is shortchanged if this is allowed to happen.

It is very difficult for me to rise to the level of higher education in this discussion. In this category, I am fully aware that in some areas, possibly most as I view it, my assessment of the route that institutions of higher learning have taken is contradictory to what I think constitutes a quality, well-rounded education. When only one side of a subject is presented, or an opposing view is not allowed to be presented without ridicule, this does not constitute a well-rounded education. When all the facts and information on a subject are presented in an impartial way, the students then have the ability to make an informed decision as to the merits of both sides. It is my perception that many teachers of today's young people enter the classroom to indoctrinate students in accepting their preconceived ideas. Many times these concepts are opposite those that have been instilled in the child since an early age which result in an inevitable conflict in the student. Both sides of an issue should be fairly taught, which would allow the student to reach a knowledgeable decision as to what is to be believed.

I can address this thought on a personal basis. My four under-graduate years were spent at Harding College (now Harding University), which is a conservative Christian university located in Searcy, Arkansas. Daily chapel attendance was a requirement, and so were Bible classes for each semester that a student was enrolled there. After receiving my degree there in 1965, I was employed for a period of time before going back to a state school in the mid-seventies to earn my master's degree in Correctional Counseling and Human Development. This involved taking psychology courses. In order to graduate, a theses paper was required on a subject of the students' choosing. Having a background in Bible, I chose to write the paper using *Psychology in the Bible* as my topic. I thought it would be of interest to show how psychology was used in the Bible to achieve certain purposes. When I presented my designated advisor with my topic request, it was immediately vetoed and I was informed that I would have to choose a different one. The reason given: "I have never read the Bible, I do not intend to read the Bible, and I would not know how to evaluate your paper. You must choose another subject." I sensed that the word Bible was enough to merit a negative response. After being accustomed to the wide range of thought encouraged for discussion in a Christian college environment, this reply came as a shock. So much for diversity in a master's degree! The outcome of the subject that was my second choice, *Disabilities in the Criminal Justice System,* proved satisfying as I received a top score with "Good paper, suitable for publication" written on it when returned. However, I was still upset over the fact that I was not able to finish my master's program in a manner of my choosing to get the well-rounded education that I felt that I deserved. I have later taken it on my own to complete my education in psychology from the Bible which I felt should have been approved when I was in school.

I dare not try to take a peek toward the future of education. There can be no denying that we have made great strides in some areas such as mathematics, science, medicine, and other important areas, and there is reason to believe that the future will lead to even greater accomplishments. History might be a different story unless there is more being taught regarding mistakes that history reveals to us which brought down mighty empires that were considered at that time to be able to stand forever. To ignore the pitfalls that resulted in the collapse of nations such as the great Roman Empire means that we are subject to such a fate. I realize that I will get poo pooed (you have to go back a ways to remember when this was used) for even suggesting that such a disaster might befall the country we love, but we must be aware of similar rumblings should they start, or already have started to make an appearance. I sincerely hope that I am wrong in suggesting that this could be our destiny. This is written not to be a forecaster of gloom and doom but a look at what will hopefully be that of a great nation that will continue to be a pioneer in what has evolved since its inception as a leader in a new found world where the land with its people are held sacred.

This is our fervent prayer. If we continue in prayers there remains the faith that they will be answered.

CHAPTER FIVE

EMPLOYMENT

Then

Physical labor was what kept food on the table as I remember things growing up. There were obviously those who had reached a higher plateau than the pick and shovel level and who lived in relative comfort, but the bulk of workers that I knew earned their living by the sweat of their brow. These were the ones who placed a biscuit and egg sandwich in their lunch pail at daybreak to return at nightfall to wash their dirty bodies clean as possible with a wet rag which had been soaked in a pan of water. Their clothes would be dirty but were worn again the next day to get even dirtier until wash day when they could be cleaned. A pair of overalls often comprised the entire selection available to the working man; two pairs were certainly a luxury, as it allowed a pair to be worn while the other one was in the washing. Long hours six days a week were expected from workers. Coal mining provided the bulk of available jobs in the area where I lived, but farming and logging also provided a source of income. Higher paying jobs such as one at a steam plant on the Black Warrior River or work on the Southern or Frisco railroads were available but limited to a fortunate few who secured them, usually those with connections. Other jobs in local cotton mills or a brick plant also provided limited employment. These jobs too were hard to get.

Back-breaking work was the order of the day. Coal was mined using picks and shovels, and in the same manner ditches were dug and dirt moved. Horses and mules were the beasts of burden pulling rail cars loaded with coal from the mines, loaded wagons filled with cargo, scoops to build and maintain roads, or plows used in farming. Horses were also used to ride on or pull wagons, buggies, and sleds for human transport. Most workers made minimal wages on which they could barely survive. The coal companies made it even more difficult by paying the worker in clacker which could only be used in their high priced commissaries. Many workers were forced to accrue debts that made them virtual servants to the company. They unwillingly did this because there were no other options.

The woman's place was in the home where she did the cooking, house cleaning, sewing, washing, and tending of children. There were often a great number of children in a household which provided a source of help as they grew up. Children were made to go to work doing chores around the home place as soon as they were able to functionally complete a task. There were always numerous things to do including the drawing and carrying of water, and cutting, stacking and carrying of stove and fire wood. Cows had to be milked and hogs and other animals fed. Milk had to be churned and vegetables picked and canned for later use. There was always an endless number of things that had to be done, and playtime did not often fit in that schedule.

I was definitely still climbing up Fools Hill when I took a job working in the cloth room at Indian Head Mills. Following a short stint there, my brother-in-law and sister who were out for the summer in college invited me to join them as they were headed to Denver, Colorado, where he had a summer job. I had never been outside the state of Alabama, and when they invited me along I jumped at the chance. They said it would be easy to get work, and it was. After a day or two, I started working for HI's Hamburgers washing dishes. Dishwashing was never one of my favorite things to do and definitely not one of my strong suits. In fact, I had never washed dishes as this was a chore that Mother and my older sisters were stuck with. The high altitude caused my nose to bleed frequently, and there was very little money to be had in the dishwashing profession. We were staying with a cousin of my brother-in-law, and after about two weeks when his wife asked what I wanted for breakfast I answered, "to eat it in Alabama." I spent what I had earned and bought a Greyhound bus ticket to Alabama. I think that I spent the money wisely.

When I returned to Alabama, jobs were hard to get and when friends who had a job catching chickens said that they needed someone to stack coops loaded with chickens onto the truck that would take them to the processing plant, I jumped at the chance to enter the poultry business. The pay would be sixty cents per thousand chickens caught. If a chicken house had ten thousand chickens, that would mean that every member of the crew would pocket six dollars. Chickens were caught at night where the darkness would restrict their movement and make them easier to catch. As they needed someone to work outside the chicken house, and as I was accustomed to lifting heavy loads when I cut and loaded timbers, I signed on. Stacking coops loaded with chickens ten or twelve high on a truck was no easy job. It was even more difficult during rainy periods. Not only did the water soaked coops weigh more, but with water collecting in coops that were already loaded with the manure from previous trips to the processing plant, tilting them in the thrust to get high enough for a high stack showered me with 90% chicken poop. I continued this for two years before it occurred to me that if chickens were to get on the table they had to be caught, but someone else would have to do the catching and stacking. Two or three of my friends came to the same conclusion, so we decided that it might be in our best interest to leave our six dollar a thousand job and get more education. Eventually, a couple from our chicken catching crew besides me got a college education, and one taught college courses as a career. He even made an appearance on a popular game quiz show where he did quite well. After those two years taking chicken poop showers, I was nearing the top of Fool's Hill and was aware of where I had gotten off track and was determined to be more cautious in accepting future job opportunities.

My salvation was when Dad took an offer to preach at a church in Osceola, Arkansas. He was offered a nice dwelling and a big increase in salary. It was quite a large house situated in a pecan grove and offered an opportunity for me to get back on track in order to top the hill. Several members of the church owned businesses, and I got several offers for employment and took one at Stead's ice cream factory. Working in an ice cream factory certainly sounded better than what I had previously been subjected to. The factory was located behind Stead's barbeque, and I filled ice cream in cartons one day and cooked pork butts the next. It was a big improvement over chicken catching.

Another church member who owned a construction company needed a truck driver to make daily trips from the construction sites to pick up building supplies in Memphis, Tennessee, and persuaded me to take that job, offering me a dollar an hour salary. That was not bad in the late 1950's, so I entered the trucking business. I did this for almost a year when the third member of the congregation who owned a dry cleaning business and needed a route sales person offered a substantial raise to what the truck driving job paid. I was plowing in high cotton now, and I developed quite a profitable route using my gift of gab. I was doing this when a fourth member who owned a well-established construction company and was quite prosperous took an interest in me and my work. He had a new Beechcraft Bonanza airplane and he would frequently invite me to ride with him as he made trips. One day he was home when I delivered his dry cleaned and washed clothes, and we had a brief conversation during which he asked why I was satisfied with a dry cleaning job when he thought that I had the potential to do better. I had filled in speaking for my father on occasions when he was away in Gospel Meetings, and apparently this man had been impressed. He inquired if I had ever considered getting a college education, and I let him know that I was saving my money to do just that. He then asked where I wanted to attend college, and when I let him know that Harding was my choice he made me an offer. He said that he would send the college $300.00 a semester to assist in my support if I wanted to attend there. He asked only one thing. I would have to give to him a picture of me in my cap and gown upon my graduation. Back then that amount of money went a long way, and with my savings I enrolled at Harding. He kept his end of the bargain, and I kept mine. After four years, I presented him a picture of me in my cap and gown which he put on his office wall. The next year he made the same offer to my brother who also gave him a graduation picture for his wall. He then helped a local Alabama boy who later became a branch manager of a local bank. I was told that he eventually had a wall filled with cap and gown pictures of graduates he had assisted in getting their education. My picture headed the line. Herman Phillips left Osceola and moved his construction business to Jonesboro, Arkansas, where he also owned shopping centers and other real estate. Throughout the years following my graduation from Harding, I kept in touch with him and let him know that I was always appreciative of his generosity. He died quite prosperous. God rewarded him for his concern for those less fortunate than he.

Now

Do not dare allow a person under the age of sixteen to do any work, or the child labor law will have you in trouble. It is permissible to allow that child to roam the streets at any hour of the day or night and pack a gun, putting that life, and others, in danger, but you better not have the audacity to put a shovel in his hand. To take away his time from the game boards and require that child to complete a simple chore is shameful. Yes, this is an overstatement but may not be too far removed from reality.

The jobs in coal mines have almost disappeared, making room for more jobs created by the electronic age. These are positions that require a better education than was needed to mine coal. Goods still must be produced, but the robot has entered the work force replacing high salaried positions that once required working hands. Employment in fast food and restaurants is in danger of being replaced by machines that can take orders and deliver food. Heavy equipment has replaced the picks and shovels, and the tractor has replaced the mule and plow. Cotton and corn are now harvested by machines and potatoes and peanuts dug mechanically. Many of the hot farm jobs that required a massive amount of labor have been replaced by chemicals and air conditioned machines that are virtually self- operated by using automated power systems guided by GPS. Long rows are straight and planted by state-of-the-art planters that sow seeds quickly with the desired spacing. Soy beans, oats, wheat, grains, and rice are now harvested in a manner not possible for the average farmer to do eighty years ago. Tractor drawn harvesting and farm equipment were unavailable to most small farmers.

One employment field that remains strong is the medical profession. This has been made possible due to the advancement of drugs that allow for a longer life span and treatment funds made available through insurance and governmental agencies. With the advancement of age comes the need for more care. The changes in this area have been drastic during my lifetime. There were no nursing homes or homes for the elderly that I can recall. The sick and terminally ill patients were cared for at home, and there they died. Medical care was sought only in an emergency. Transportation to a hospital was provided by anyone who had an available vehicle that could be used for transport. Ambulances were either not available or in very short supply. Hospital care was rejected by many who preferred to peacefully die at home.

Recently, I was in a hospital when a young boy entered the emergency room seeking treatment for a small cut on his finger. As a boy I would just have washed the blood off it and continued to do whatever I was doing. A splinter or briar embedded in flesh was removed by knife point or needle when I was young. Today a trip to the emergency room is the standard for its removal. I recently overheard a woman telling another about the emergency trip she had recently made to the hospital. The emergency: she had found a tick on her daughter, and it had to be removed. Ambulances are summoned and patients are rushed to hospitals, sirens and light blaring, because the person all of a sudden felt a little "dizzy- headed" and thought it best to have a doctor check them out. Someone else will pay the bill anyway so why not be safe? There is no wonder that jobs and pay in the health field have skyrocketed in the modern era.

What will the next eighty years bring in the medical field? Will there be those at that time who will be considered young at age eighty? What will the next eighty years usher in in the form of jobs? Only time will answer this. As this is written the age of drones has begun to make deliveries and do other chores. Will drones be the next delivery boy for drugs? Advancements occur so rapidly that by the time this writing goes to print some of the questions we might have regarding this will already be answered. We probably, as did those eighty years ago, have no concept of what the workforce will look like after the next eighty years have passed. What will be the latest method of transporting medical emergencies to the treatment centers?

If any trend has been set during my lifetime, it is that a sound education will be the key to having a good job in the future. The picks and shovels will never return. The cotton pickers will not return to the fields. Coal will be replaced by natural gas or a renewable energy which brings on the closing of the mines that offered jobs to so many in the past. Robots and automation will continue to replace the work of individuals. It will be the worker who is able to adapt to these changes that will be able to be effective in the new fields that will open up, and that worker will have the advantage in securing employment.

CHAPTER SIX

TRANSPORTATION

Then

This subject stands out to me as having made the greatest changes in my lifetime. I attribute this to the fact that from having very limited transportation except on a school bus or riding my thumb, walking was the sole way that I could go beyond the confines of my tiny world at the end of the road. School buses only carried me to and from school, and walking had a limited range to get me to a desired destination. My thumb, however, transported me thousands of miles. "Thumbing" was a standard means for one to travel at that time. To get to an early morning job that I had secured at the local five and dime store, I left before the school bus ran, as I had chores to do such as clean floors and shelves and roll out the front awning before the store opened at eight a.m. At that time hitchhiking was a reliable means of transportation. Much of the time I would be able to get repeated rides from individuals who made the trip to town every day at the time I was hitchhiking. After graduation I continued to use this method to travel both inside and out of the state. During that time I never felt threatened for my safety but did meet many interesting characters, but that is for another book.

My dad always owned a vehicle; none were reliable enough to venture away any long distance. He always bought them used, and he had a knack for finding the ones that had the most use and were ready for retirement. On one occasion he lucked out and bought a Studebaker truck that was immune to abuse. All six of us kids would climb into the truck's bed, rain or shine, with Dad always doing the driving and away we would go. Mother never drove a mile in her life that I am aware of. That, too, was typical of the times in which I was raised.

There was a nearby country store at the intersection which sold gasoline where our road left the main road. Gas was delivered to the cars by means of hand pumping the desired amount into an overhead marked tank and then fed into the gas tank of the car by gravity until the marked tank had emptied. It was a day to be remembered when pumps were installed that pulled the gas directly from the underground tanks that metered the gas as it went through the nozzle. Standard Oil filled the underground tanks, one with super and the other with regular leaded gasoline which was then pumped from two different tanks. The day when the tanks first came into service and we filled our car's tank from them for the first time, for some strange reason, remains stored in my memory bank. All of us kids wanted to be the first to put the nozzle in the car's gas tank opening and pump the gas, but Dad insisted on doing the honors. Transportation had reached another milestone in making travel by automobile more convenient.

The condition of country roads was another factor that entered into the mix of determining whether or not a trip by automobile would be an enjoyable one. There were road crews who would try to get around to scraping a road once a year or so, but this did not prevent bad roads from playing havoc when they were muddy. There were rural farmers who made extra spending money by using their horses or mules to free a stuck vehicle. The expert drivers could usually hit the ruts in such a way as to pass through successfully, but others would fall victim to the mire that the road had become.

Dust was another problem. After the roads had dried out, they became very dusty. Most cars were not air tight and clothes being worn by those in the car would receive a dusty covering. There were no air conditioned cars, and if the windows were closed it became very hot and stuffy inside, but if the windows were down another layer of dust would be deposited inside with every passing car that kicked up another round of dust. Dust also created a hazard as approaching cars were difficult to see though the dust, thus becoming the cause of many accidents. My father was involved in one such dust created accident. He had made the mistake of buying a tan colored car which the approaching driver did not see until it was too late to avoid contact. Those houses that stood alongside a dirt road were forced to endure a long summer of constant dusty conditions. The rains then brought muddy conditions, but this had more of an adverse effect on those traveling the roads than it did on the ones who lived beside it. At least the dust was settled until the next dry spell.

The different means of available travel were just emerging from their primitive state when I was born. Public transportation had reached its height and was beginning to wane as more people bought and used automobiles as their sole means of transportation. Train travel was still popular, and there were still "whistle stops" at every community that bordered the railroads. At that time there were only steam engines pulling the cars, and it was not difficult to know when the passenger train was approaching as there would always be a lot of smoke, a shrill whistle, and the sounds that were emitted from the belching beast. One would stand by the tracks at whistle stops and, as the train approached, a wave of the hand would grant admittance. The conductor would collect a small toll, and you would be on your way to your destination. It would be only a short time until the locomotive would be replaced, and the passenger trains would find their final resting place along an abandoned spur line. There they met their fate, most to be scrapped to find a new life molded into a modern version of train cars and other vehicles. Steam engines would succumb to more powerful diesel work horses, and the coal miners who supplied fuel for their furnaces would be replaced by workers in the oil fields.

Greyhound made daily routes, and the locals had a station in every sizable town. Express routes had stops only in the larger towns and were the accepted means of travel for the passenger who was in a hurry. A local stopped at every crossroads, and it took forever to reach your intended destination. Unless you were traveling a long distance, that would be your ride. In order for a business to send or receive packages that needed to be delivered quickly, the Greyhound would perform that task and deliver it as soon as it arrived in the designated town. Many times I heard about an item that was needed quickly, "It will be here on the next bus". Sometimes there would be as many people, or more, waiting at the station to pick up cargo as there would be for those who greeted guests. Greyhound had their competitors, but Greyhound was the name that people connected to bus lines. Buses were often filled to capacity and latecomers were forced to wait until the arrival of the next bus. For a period of time a local bus line aptly named Misala Stages, as the route traveled extended from Alabama into towns in Eastern Mississippi, did a booming business. Radio ads gave the time schedule from Jasper to Birmingham as leaving every hour on the hour. This line did business for a number of years until the ridership fell, and the second or third generation of buses wore out. The point was reached where it was no longer a profitable business, and the age of buses in our area slowly yielded to changing times and disappeared into history. Following that, automobiles reigned supreme.

During this period of time, the major companies that manufactured automobiles were very competitive in marketing their products. Some brands such as Nash, Hudson, Studebaker, Packard, Kaiser, Frazer, and others appeared, survived for a while, and then disappeared. The major three companies, Ford, General Motors, and Chrysler were challenged for a long time by American Motors, but it was absorbed by a competing company and it too was relegated to history. Even the three major companies produced models that were flops. High on this list were Ford's Edsel, Chrysler's Valiant, and General Motor's rear engine Corvair. The Gremlin did little to help American Motors survive. The German Volkswagen bug made its appearance following the war and became quite popular. The Yugo made in Czechoslovakia was a bust. Advertised to be the answer to cheap transportation, it was not long before those who had been willing to give them a try understood why they were sold so cheaply: they soon fell apart, and parts were not readily available.

Yearly model changes from the big three companies gave each model a brand new look. When young, I would stand by the main road where we caught the school bus and be able to identify every passing car by make and year model. When a late model expensive car would pass, I would dream of owning one like it one day--so were the wishes of a stranded country boy who yearned to travel to faraway places but conceded that these were unachievable dreams.

Now

As I sit at my computer and write this sentence, I have my feet under a table in Timisoara, Romania. In two days, I plan to board a plane and return to my home in Alabama. The flight schedule lists a departure time of 6:05 A.M. and an arrival of approximately the same time in the

P.M in Huntsville, Alabama. We will leave Romania after the sun rises and will be in Huntsville before the sun sets, as we will fly with the sun and gain back the eight hours we lost traveling to get here with a six hour layover in Munich, Germany factored in. The thought that this could be accomplished would have been unbelievable in my childhood. I have repeated this scenario numerous times traveling to many parts of the world. The country boy's dream has materialized, and the faraway places are now only a sunlit day away.

I can still recall the first time I was made aware that there was an aircraft that did not even need a runway. I learned that it was called a helicopter, and it could take off going straight up and hover. It could lift heavy loads and land on almost any level clearing. It was capable of conducting rescue operations which would have been impossible before. Sightseers had a method of flying slow and low over pictur-esque terrain, and law enforcement had a new method of surveillance, investigation of illegal activities, and doing an array of other duties. The helicopter became a helpful tool for filming movies and other photo-graphic assignments. It has become an important tool in the military arsenal credited for saving the lives of many of our military personnel.

Obviously, the world of transportation has made drastic changes in my lifetime. I would never dare to attempt to hitchhike now, even around a city block, nor would the average person consider picking me up and allowing me to enter their vehicle. There are no passenger trains that even come near our neck of the woods, and the few Greyhound buses that still may be running near us fly by on the interstate never slowing to under seventy miles an hour. If I should stand on the road-side and try to identify the make and model of passing cars, I would have three strikes against me after the passing of the first three. They all practically look alike to me except for colors. We have been invaded by cars wearing foreign names and models and which now have a respect-able share of the market. The domestic auto makers allowed this to happen when there was a period of time that they put an inferior prod-uct on the market, and the people were drawn to the superior exported cars, Japan being a leader.

One of the greatest accomplishments that came out of the Eisen-hower Presidency was the Interstate Highway Program. This is one of the greatest advancements that have allowed rapid access to any part of the nation without any stops or barriers. This has allowed not only passengers but cargo to move freely from coast to coast. President Eisenhower brought the plan from Germany after observing how their Autobahn made travel much easier. Muddy and dusty roads are virtually a thing of the past in this country. Having experienced the problem which bad roads can cause, I put it high on the list of improvements that we as a nation have accomplished.

Cars and trucks are now more reliable than ever. Constant improvements have been made through the years, and the expected reliability of an automobile has more than doubled during that time. Once, for a vehicle to serve reliably for 100,000 miles was pushing the limits of ownership and serviceability. Now, in my experience, a well maintained vehicle can easily be expected to run two or three times that amount of mileage. I can recall problems with starters, alternators, radiators, blown head gaskets, fuel pumps and an array of other problems that were expected should the vehicle run for the 100,000 miles. Now these problems have been virtually eliminated. Radial tires and tubeless tires have replaced the old tube type bias ones which have greatly extended mileage and reliability. Automatic transmissions and air conditioners, at first a costly option when buying a new car, are now standard equipment. Power windows, door locks, rear view mirrors, tilt seats, and various other power features are all included in a package that does almost everything but drive the car. And we must include the GPS, rear view camera for safe backing, compass, thermometer, and gages that tell the driver everything but the price of gasoline at the nearest station, but I suspect that is in the works and near completion. Cars now require keys that can lock or unlock and even crank a car from outside, activate an alarm, and do all this at a distance, or just keep the key in your pocket, the car will crank with the push of a button if the key is in close proximity. Power steering and cruise control have taken much of the effort out of driving. Expected gas mileage has improved and electric cars are trying to nudge their way into the fleet. Self-driving cars are being tested and will also be seeking a share of the market. Where will all this lead? I suspect that even those who are building them would be hard pressed to answer this question.

CHAPTER SEVEN

POLITICS

Then

Pardon me while I pause and put on a pair of overalls, roll up the legs, and put on my wading shoes. When I grew up in Alabama, I was not aware that the word dirty and the word politics were two separate words. There was always talk that the moonshiners had to work overtime in order to supply the demand created by the politicians. We lived in a rural area and there was the continual accusation that the winner of a political race was able to supply more "shine" to the county voters than the other candidates. Now this is not intended to be an accusation against those politicians of long ago but merely a mention of those making these assertions that were supposedly in the know. Seeing that those who were actually making the claims were the defeated candidates, this accusation might be taken with a grain of salt and might not be entirely the case. Now you do understand that we are talking politics here and anything goes! Nevertheless, I feel more comfortable discussing this with my overalls on and ready to wade when I have swamps to cross. Politics is not one of my favorite subjects to discuss.

Thanks to my father, we were shielded from the mudslinging by his completely avoiding involvement in the political process. Not once during my elementary and high school days do I remember him even discussing politics. During that time I never knew of him voting or endorsing candidates. I can almost say with a certainty that he was not even registered to vote. He would never have paid the poll tax that was required at that time. Putting food on the table was a higher priority than paying to be able to vote. Alabama had a poll tax of $1.50 a year (over $11.00 in today's dollars) which was required before one could register to vote. On March 3rd of 1966 Federal courts declared the poll tax to be unconstitutional in Alabama in state elections thus ending the requirement that one must pay in order to vote. The 24th amendment ratified in 1964, had already abolished the use of the poll tax in Federal elections. This tax had been enacted not only for revenue sources but to restrict the participation of blacks and the lower class in the political arena. Literacy tests were also a requirement for some before they were allowed to vote. This was also abolished in part by the Voting Rights Act of 1965 and completely by the Supreme Court in 1970. When I was young it cost to be a voting citizen in this country, and if you were considered to be second class or undesirable you didn't. So much for free political expression in America!

Democrats could rely on the "solid South" to support their candidate. Those who were running in national elections rarely campaigned in general elections in Alabama because they knew that the South was already in their corner. If Satan ran for an office as a Democrat he would beat a Republican by a landslide. Yellow Dog Democrats were true to their party no matter who their candidate might be. This applied to national, state, and local candidates. All the well-known national leaders from Alabama in that era were members of the Democratic Party.

As stated, Dad did not get involved in voting. He however was known to express his opinion as to the performance of those in office. Franklin D. Roosevelt was the President when I was born and Dad thought he was the best to have ever held that office. When Dad was young he, as did the masses, suffered through the Great Depression which was a traumatic experience for a young boy whose mother was dead and father living the life of a hobo. He was bounced from pillar to post and dependent upon anyone who would barter a day's food for a day's work no matter how meager the food offering might be. Dad saw FDR as the savior who pulled the nation out of chaos, and he frequently spoke highly of him. He had praise for the programs he instituted to fight poverty and he praised the building of TVA dams and power plants. FDR was a Democrat that Dad praised, yet the one who followed Roosevelt, Harry S. Truman, did not fill the standards

Dad felt that the President of the United States should possess. He considered him to be a vile man who was, as best as I can recall, prone to the use of profanity. He was not very high on Margaret, his daughter, either. The next president, Dwight D. Eisenhower, a Republican, met Dad's approval and was a good president. Democrat or Republican, Dad judged a politician by his performance in office. It might be noted that I used the masculine gender as I never knew of a female politician at that time. Politics was a man's world, and the females stayed at home and raised their children.

During election time, utility poles were the politician's best friend. Almost every pole in plain sight had campaign posters tacked to it. Later it was signs tacked on wooden strips that cluttered the roadside with every intersection infested with them like ticks on a hound dog. No matter that it was declared illegal, hey, we are talking about politicians here; they considered themselves to be above the law. Should we wonder why their performance in office has been no better and we are presently in the dismal shape that we are in today? We, in our local county, have been warned that bankruptcy is looming in the near future. A one-cent sales tax election was called and defeated because the politicians were not trusted to spend the additional revenue wisely, based on their predecessor's past performances that led to the crisis. Some things have been inherited from long ago and today's politicians apparently were poor history students and never seem to understand that they cannot give their constituents everything they want and keep their finances afloat. Oh well, we understand the rationale behind their actions; they do what is necessary to be re-elected so they can make some more bone-headed moves.

When we go back to the methods used by politicians in local elections, there was more direct contact with the voters then than now. It was expected that there be personal contact with the voter, or a card left in the door of all the houses in the district. If the candidate did not have enough support to enlist an army of volunteers to do foot work for him, he was at a disadvantage. Volunteers tacked up campaign posters, went door to door with literature, stood at intersections holding signs and stuck bumper stickers on every car that would accept them. One of the most memorable bumper stickers was "Y'all Come" which everyone knew was an endorsement of Big Jim Folsom, a popular although reportedly corrupt governor. Candidates would mount large speakers on the roofs of their cars or pickups, blaring a solicitation to cast a vote for them and announcing the time and place where they would be holding a political rally. At the rally there would be volunteers in the crowd passing out literature in support of the candidate. Campaign buttons bearing the name of the candidate and the office he was seeking were also a popular item.

Now

If aspiring candidates do not have the financial backing now, they had better stay on the sidelines. The name of the game in politics now is MONEY, MONEY, MONEY! It does not matter that the repetitive mud-slinging ads on T.V. become so irritating that one finally can no longer bear them and refuses to watch; this is where political campaigns have come in today's electronic world. It is generally accepted that the candidate with the largest amount of funds to use in a campaign has the advantage over lesser funded opponents. Incumbents who have done a decent job, and some who have not, also have an advantage.

In many ways, the political scene is much different than it was eighty years ago. Females are now in the picture and hold many of the elective offices once dominated by males, and some do as good or a better job than the males. Blacks, who were once barred from voting, now have the same opportunities to be elected as does anyone else. Many of the large cities such as Birmingham, Alabama, which once suppressed their black citizens, are now governed by them, and they are in the majority. A black President has now served our nation. A female was the nominee of the Democrats and ran for President of the United States.

The South is still the solid South but the color has changed from blue to red on the political map. Where Democrats once held the upper hand, Republicans are now in control. It is now the Republican candidates for national elections who do not bother to spend time in the Southern states, with Florida being the exception. Now everyone is either labeled as being a liberal or conservative, and it is this designation that has caused the switch in political parties in the South. The conservative viewpoint is dominant among the Southern populous, and therefore the individual who holds these views is the one who will be elected. Many of the old die-hard Democrats bemoan the fact that their party has left them in their convictions, and they either fail to vote or reluctantly mark one for the Republican candidate of their choice. Many of the politicians who were elected when the Democrats were in power have switched parties, as they no longer can endorse its platform and know that their political lives depend on being in the dominate party.

When I was young, there were no political polls to inform the citizenry about the latest scoop on the frontrunner in the race and how people felt about his positions. They have yet to figure out how to make them to be a pertinent forecaster of the eventual winner of a race. Too often, polls appear to be slanted toward the favored candidate of the ones conducting the polls. This is done by the way questions asked in the poll are formulated, giving an advantage to the politician who holds their views. Individually, I have never found any value in political polls and put no trust in their accuracy.

At the time of this writing the political climate is so unsettled that it is anyone's guess as to what the future holds for either party. Will one become dominant nationally over the other as has happened in the South? Will minorities and immigrants play a deciding role in future elections? Will third party voters gain enough of a foothold to make their voices heard and be a factor in future elections? The electorate is so divided that the future looks bleak that there will be any less turmoil in the coming elections than has been displayed in recent ones. There are a lot of unknowns, which only the passing of time will reveal.

CHAPTER EIGHT

ENTERTAINMENT/RECREATION

Then

Of one thing I can be certain, if there was anyone who had an idea that they could successfully open an exercise gym around my childhood home place back then and expect it to be profitable, they would have been laughed out of town. After all the chores were completed and it was bedtime, there would not have been enough energy left in one's body to open the door to the place. Weight lifting was accomplished by lifting firewood and carrying it into the house, cutting and loading timbers, carrying 100 pound sacks of animal feed, lugging water from the well or creek, and numerous other household chores. Drawing water from the well provided a means to exercise arm muscles. There were more than enough errands to run to build up the leg muscles and to keep one in good physical shape. After homework from school was completed, one was ready to "hit the sack." Roosters would announce a new day very early in the morning when a new day of activities would begin.

There was very little time for play when I was growing up. My brother and I were introduced to a crosscut saw when we were old enough to use it, and we cut pulpwood and mining timbers from our land to help with needed expenses. There was always work to do around the home place which required most of our time. We had no bicycles to ride or balls with which to play. Well, scratch that, as we did have a bicycle. I hesitate to call it a bicycle because it was nothing but a frame and wheels. It had no fenders and the chain did not work. It had only one pedal and no brakes. The only way to ride it was to push it to the top of a hill, jump on, and hang on. This is the way that I learned to ride a bicycle, but not without an ample share of scrapes and bruises. In regard to the lack of balls to play with, I can recall that we once used a hog's bladder for a football and twine wrapped around a black walnut for a baseball; a sturdy stick served as a bat. We were not exactly in the big league!

When with other children, there were games we played such as hide and go seek, follow the leader, hopscotch, dodge ball (if we could find a ball to use), Annie over (involved throwing a ball over a building), Mumble peg (a boys game that involved throwing a knife from different parts of the body and have it stick upright in the ground), and marbles. Many marble games were played for keeps which allowed the shooter to keep any marble he knocked outside the ring. A taw was what the marble players used to shoot with their thumbs to knock other marbles from the ring. There were always horseshoes to pitch to ring the stake in the ground or washers to land in one of the three lined holes that were dug in order to play the game. Horseshoes were pitched with vocabulary such as ringers and leaners. Horseshoes were not hard to come by as there were normally used and extra ones at the barn. Also pitched were washers, although I recall that when some of our more prosperous relatives visited they liked to show off by using silver dollars in place of washers. In both the games of horseshoes and washers opposing sides stood a distance facing each other and with horseshoes the participants attempted to ring a stake set in the ground on the opposition side. With washers there were three small round holes hardly bigger than the washers dug in a reversing row, one as near the next as possible. They were dug on each side, and the object of the game was to throw the washer so as to ring the hole. There were more points to be earned by ringing the back hole than putting the washer in the first. A washer in the first hole was worth 5 points, the second 10 points, and the third 15 (or 20, if so decided). These were outdoor activities, but there were games to be played on a rainy day. The "show-offs" would drag out a chess board in order to display their expertise, while those who just wanted to have a simpler game would opt for dominoes, checkers, Rook or Old Maid cards (playing cards were not allowed in many households, including ours), Chinese checkers, pick-up-sticks, tic-tac-toe, and various board games if available.

Daddy at one time built us a flying jenny which was fun but potentially dangerous. The construction involved cutting down a large tree leaving a high stump. A twelve foot long 2 by 8 inch board was then attached to the top of the stump in a way that allowed the board to spin. An application of a little axle grease between the board and the stump would enable the board to rotate very fast. Caution had to be taken so as not to get into the path of the spinning board. See-saws were made by placing the boards over a fallen log. Sometimes two of the smaller children had to get on one end to counter-balance the weight of the larger person.

When small, we would play cars with any object we could push around in the dirt. We would push out roads to drive our vehicles on, and when the car was in motion we would make a sound with our lips to imitate the sound of a running motor. I still remember that my first play car was no car at all. It was a piece of iron that had been used to secure a barn door. It was shaped in such a way that it could be fastened on one side of the door. Another like it on the other side allowed a heavy board to be inserted between the two across the front of the door which was an effective bar to keep the door closed. Country boys made do with what they could find while using a little imagination.

We had an old mule named Dock that pulled a plow in order for us to make a garden. Dock would not let anyone ride him, and those who tried ended up being unceremoniously expelled from his back. We did find a way to use him to have fun. We built a sled and would hitch him to it and ride. We had trails through the woods which we had worn while riding the sled. Another way we used a sled, or slides as we called them, was on what we named "straw hill." This ride did not involve old Dock but was more like a roller derby with no wheels; maybe we could call it a sliding derby. There was a rather steep slope covered with pine needles which at the bottom gently curved upward to an adjoining hill. We spent many hours on straw hill riding our slides. The thick pine needles made the perfect runway to send our slides racing down the hill. We each made our own slides and we would have races to see which was the fastest. As stated, boys who lived in the country could find ways to amuse themselves.

Entertainment outside our little sphere was almost non-existent. The last three years I was in high school, I was a member of the marching band and was able to attend football games without having to pay admission. Professional sports were not available, and I never attended a movie until my senior year, when I was able to view *Twenty Thousand Leagues under the Sea* as I have already mentioned. The majority of our outside related activities involved church services and gospel singings. Fishing, trapping, digging ginseng, and other outdoor activities provided enjoyable pursuits that occupied the little bit of spare time that was available for me. Televisions had not yet made their appearance in our little po-dunk community during my early childhood, and we did not own one during most of my early years. We did own a radio, but the static was so bad that it was difficult to stay tuned to an entire program.

Swimming holes were few and far between on our dry section of land, but there was one where water channeled through a railroad culvert poured into a small creek. We frequented that as often as possible. There was a railroad trestle over the Warrior River three or four miles from the house, and we would sometimes walk to it to join others who jumped from the bridge to the water below. It was quite a distance from the tracks to the water, and we were warned about the danger involved in the jump. Boys will be boys, however, and we would sneak off and go and jump from the bridge. The problem with this was that we would almost always return home with our swimsuits covered with creosote that the heat had drawn from the treated crossties we had sat on, and then the gig was up when it came to facing Momma. There was an advantage, however, after the first application of creosote to our swim trunks. The stuff was there on a permanent basis and as we only had one pair, we had to wear them with the creosote decoration on them. The advantage there was that Mother could not always tell when additional applications of the stuff were added, so it was easier to go jump off the bridge without getting caught. One had to figure every angle in order to be an accomplished deceiver of forbidden activities. For those not in the know, that stuff won't come out of clothing, and around our house clothing was scarce. I am still amazed that I was able to climb Fool's Hill safely. Considering some of the dare-devil capers I pulled, God must have provided me with a special Guardian Angel.

Eventually Dad had a pond dug in our bottom land ("the bottoms," as we referred to it) and the problem of finding a swimming hole was solved. No matter that after a little splashing around the clear water would become dingy with mud from the bottom, water is water and that was one way to cool off after a hard day's work or on a leisurely Sunday afternoon. The pond served as a magnet for neighborhood children.

Radio was one way that we could find entertainment if we could get anything worthwhile through the static. There were thousands of radio shows that came and went, but there were some that I listened to and which I still remember. For some strange reason, several of the names of those shows still linger in my mind, and as this writing is an attempt to drain my memory bank I am going to pull out as many of them that I remember and write their names here. The program we listened to most often was the *Grand Ole Opry*. On Saturday night, we as a family would gather around the radio to listen to our favorite country stars perform. Minnie Pearl always brought a laugh, as did Grandpa Jones and String Bean. Bear with me while I jot down some of my favorites: Hank Snow, Tex Ritter, Roy Clark, Sonny James, Porter Wagoner, Hank Williams, Chet Atkins, Roy Acuff, Eddie Arnold, Red Foley, Johnny and June Carter Cash, Lester Flatts, Kitty Wells, Earl Scruggs, George Jones, Marty Robbins, Ferlin Husky, Earnest Tubbs; and don't forget Box Car Willie. There were hundreds of other performers, some of whom may have been your favorites. Most of the members of the *Grand Ole Opry* now were not performing when I listened to the program years ago. Conversely, the majority of those who did perform at that time have left their musical instruments to be included in museums and have gone on to their rewards. There are always those who are eager to replace them.

Of the many radio shows that aired before television caused their demise, there are a number that I recall as being the most interesting to me. Again I will jot some of them down. As I ponder through my memory bank, I am thinking that this list might be somewhat lengthy. I will start by saying that I can vividly recall listening to *The Green Hornet* one night when I was alone at home. It was a scary episode and right at the end when you learned what happened, the static wiped out the entire ending. I was scared by the story which was unfolding and stayed scared until I was no longer alone.

My dad's favorites were *Lum and Abner, Amos and Andy, Abbott and Costello, Cab Calloway, Jack Benny, Red Skelton, Fibber McGee and Molly,* and *George Burns and Gracie Allen.* Having only one radio, we listened to a lot of what Dad wanted to hear. The girls had their favorites, too. If given a chance they would listen to *Our Miss Brooks, Breakfast in Hollywood, Little Orphan Annie, Ozzie and Harriet, The Original Amateur Hour, Our Miss Brooks, Queen for a Day, This Is Your Life, People are Funny* and *Mickey Mouse.*

We boys had a number of favorites; most of them involved a lot of action. Some were *The Lone Ranger, Roy Rogers* (king of the cowboys), *Gunsmoke, Gene Autry, Have Gun will Travel, Dragnet, The Green Hornet,* and *Red Ryder.* There were also dramas and mysteries such as *Yours Truly, Johnny Dollar, Orson Wells,* and *The Mercury Theater on the air, Inter-Sanctum, Sergeant Preston of the Yukon, Whistler,* and *Boston Blackie.*

When we finally got a Crosby 19-inch TV, black and white of course, we were then able to watch some of the same programs, but they never had the same impact on the imagination as did those radio shows. On television we enjoyed watching the old cowboy and Indian and western movies where the good guys always wore the white hats and the bad guys wore black. The good guys always won. Some of the carry-overs from radio that we did like were *Gunsmoke, Have Gun will Travel, Roy Rogers, Sargent Preston of the Yukon,* and *Dragnet.* The girls watched *Our Miss Brooks, This is Your Life, People Are Funny,* and *Mickey Mouse.*

Now

Don't throw away that box that the toy came in. The kids had rather play with it than the toy itself. Go to almost any kid's room today, and you will practically have to wade through the toys, some of which have probably seen little playing time. Wait until Christmas and there will be another layer on the one that has just been added at the birthday party. Not for one to worry though, the toy companies will advertise one that the youngsters must have, and you will not need to wait for a special occasion to add that one to the pile. In the end, the one that will occupy all of your kid's time will be an electronic device that will do anything but clean up the child's room after all those toys have been thrown in the floor and then ignored.

I recall how kids would be outdoors in mass in pretty weather playing sports, riding bicycles, or just enjoying being outside. I do not see that much anymore. It is now preferable to sit inside in comfort and devote time to playing games on electronic devices. It seems now that many young people are not willing to devote the energy needed to exercise their bodies.

Thriving businesses now are personal fitness establishments and programs that provide an opportunity to get the exercise that the body needs. In my eighty years of life, I have observed desk jobs replacing those requiring physical labor, and weights and treadmills have taken the place of fire logs and errands. Jogging tracks also serve to provide a means to provide exercise for legs and body. Many make frequent golf outings that also provide exercise and entertainment.

Gone are the days when anyone could find it to be problematic to find some type of entertainment. Television, golf, sports, movies, hunting, fishing (in expensive boats and tackle), travel: the list is endless. Many will become tired of what is now available to them and expect new and exciting ways to be entertained. How the future can improve on this is anyone's guess. You can be certain that there are efforts being made at this time to do just that. There have been great successes in achieving this in my lifetime. Will the playing fields be any different after eighty more years have passed?

Another change that has occurred over the passing of time in the field of entertainment is amusement events, and parks. In Walker County each year, many looked forward to the Northwest Alabama Fair coming to town. Kids would save money so as to be able to ride the Ferris wheel, bumper cars, tilt-a-whirl, merry-go-round, and other rides. Many were determined to leave with a prize won by various skill games, some con games, not realizing that the cards were stacked against them by unscrupulous operators. There were always side shows featuring humans, or animals, with a grotesque abnormality, which barkers would proclaim to be one of a kind.

Vendors would provide cotton candy, shaved ice, soft drinks, lemonade, hotdog, hamburgers, and various other food items to appease the appetite. Housewives would spend months preparing to enter their quilts, canned goods, clothing, and other things, hoping to win a blue ribbon. Students in 4-H would bring their projects in for judging, as did farmers with their cattle, chickens, watermelons, pumpkins, fruit and vegetables, all in quest of the blue ribbon.

The State fair in Birmingham was always a big event, although we poor kids never got the opportunity to enjoy it, as the distance and cost was prohibitive to a family of eight.

Fast forward to now and there have been changes. State and county fairs have had their heyday and have either been downsized or eliminated. Amusement parks such as Six Flag, Opryland, and Alabama Adventure, provided a complete summer of activities on a larger scale than the traveling carnivals. Water parks now offer refreshments and fun to avoid the summer's heat.

Over the passing of time, some of these amusement parks, such as Opryland, have come and gone. Increasing inflation has made the property on which they were located more valuable. Hotels, public buildings, conference centers, and shopping centers now occupy the sites where there were once screaming kids enjoying their rides.

Such is the nature of progress; it would be interesting to be able to return after eighty more years have passed to see what occupies the sites then. We might be in awe as to the changes. Of one thing I feel we can be sure, it will be a far cry from the county fairs of my youth.

With the advancements of the space age will it be that a trip into space be made possible for the masses? I am told that already there have been those who have made reservation and a deposit on space travel. Some even anticipate that they will be able to visit a colony having been established on the moon. As we ponder the possibilities of this occurring, remember that if we go back only a little more than fifty years, the possibilities of man walking on the moon seemed a very remote possibility.

It is also interesting to ponder what toy, or electronic gadget, will be in the hands of the youngsters at that time. Will young girls still cuddle their dolls, or will dolls, as have many other children's toys, be forsaken for new and different playthings? People will find ways to be entertained, and the possibility that the methods of entertainment that I grew up with will soon be forgotten.

CHAPTER NINE

COMFORT/FOOD

Then

Hardships were expected and realized in the 1930's and 40's. Summers were going to be hot as they have always been and winters cold. Enduring this was still a way of life, and preparation was made to survive during the changing of the seasons. In the hot summertime there was sweat to be wiped as one stood holding plow handles behind a horse or mule while growing fields of corn, potatoes, and vegetables to be saved for the winter months. Wives and children prepared the produce, and women stood over the hot wood stove doing canning in jars to preserve the needed food to last until the next crop was raised. Fire in the cook stove had to be maintained, and this involved the cutting and bringing in of firewood. This job was regularly relegated to the children. Storage space, often in a basement or cellar, was necessary to properly store the canned goods to prevent freezing during the cold days ahead.

The woods and fields yielded a bounty if an effort was made to take advantage of it. Fruit trees were often planted, and dried apples were often turned into tasty turnovers, which the accomplished cook could use to make any mouth water. Apples were cored, peeled, sliced, and then spread out in the sun on a sheet to dry. The task was to keep bees and yellow jackets off them until they had time to dry. This was often accomplished by spreading a thin second sheet over the drying fruit. Peaches were canned or pickled in canning jars. Pears were made into preserves and made a good breakfast food when served with butter and biscuits. Available blackberries were almost always expected to be picked and preserved. This often was a family affair with the children expected to do their share in the pickings. Caution always had to be taken as a blackberry patch was often the favorite habitat of copperhead snakes. Blackberry vines also afforded wasps a good place to build their nests, and they did not take too kindly to being disturbed. Long sleeves in the boiling sun were required due to the briars that guarded the berries from being picked. After picking, fingers and hands would be stained due to the juice from overripe blackberries, and those stains would last for days. Inevitably briars would scratch hands that picked the berries from the thorny vines leaving those hands in an unsightly condition. There was certainly no comfort to be had in a blackberry patch. The efforts of picking them, however, were certainly rewarded. An early morning breakfast that included blackberry jelly or jam with butter and biscuits was a great way to start the day. A blackberry cobbler that topped off a dinner of vegetables cooked from the pantry was about as good as it could get. The effort put into picking the berries was soon forgotten.

We always kept a milk cow, but at times she would go dry after being bred and was carrying a calf. At those times we would buy sweet milk and buttermilk from Mom's aunt, but it was a distance to travel to get whole milk, and we often turned to Carnation or Pet milk as a substitute. Mother would mix it with about three times as much water as recommended, and we became accustomed to watered down, canned milk. Milk was not the only thing that Mother would be extra generous with water when mixing. I can remember that one day when I happened to read the mixing directions on the label of a can of Campbell's soup, I could not believe that the instructions were for mixing a can of soup with a can of water. It always took two or three cans of soup to feed the family but Mother would mix it with three or four times the amount of water that the directions called for. She had hungry mouths to feed, and we did not complain because we didn't know the difference. At least the water was flavored quite well.

It has to be remembered that there was no freezer in which to preserve the food needed for wintertime, nor did we have a refrigerator until I was a young teenager. It was a General Electric and that thing lasted forever. We eventually got a chest type freezer which took much of the burden of canning food away from Mom, although there were certain things such as jams, jellies, pickles, preserves, and juices which still went into jars. One of the biggest advantages of having a freezer was that now there was a way to store meat without it spoiling. We always raised hogs to be killed after the weather had turned cold. The pork was well salted and placed in a smoke house and allowed to cure. With the freezer, hog or beef killing time was more flexible. Rarely did Dad buy meat on the market.

Chickens were raised free range and roosters provided meat when needed. Hens were free to lay their eggs anywhere they chose to make a nest, and one of the fun things to do was to look for and find a hen's nest and gather the eggs. Hens would always cackle after laying which offered a clue as to where to look for a nest. At times a mother hen would show up with a number of "bitties," as we called them, in tow having successfully hidden her nest giving the eggs time to hatch. We typically had Rhode Island Reds, Plymouth Rock, Leghorns Bantams and Dominique chickens. The Leghorns were probably the best layers and they were the breed that we commonly had, along with a lot of Bantams. The Dominique breed tended to have a mean streak in their nature, and I recall a Dominique rooster that was downright hostile. Perhaps it was for this reason that the breed, which is considered to be the oldest in the USA, fell out of favor. Therefore, recently, their number dwindled to around five-hundred who still survive.

Guinea hens were always on the homestead, for what reason I have no idea. I will concede that they will give a dog a run for the money when it comes to announcing an intruder. We never ate one, nor did we eat their eggs. As we did not gather their eggs, we accumulated quite a flock of them and it was well know that if someone wanted Guinea hens, we were the supplier. They were always given free to the recipient. As I recall, there were not a whole lot of people who desired to have a Guinea. As we lived at road's end, and had fifty-six acres for our animals to roam, we offered quite a sanctuary for our animals.

Field corn was widely grown back then both for human and animal consumption. The Mosby variety was always Dad's favorite, and that was what he planted. When it was ready to be harvested, we would pick it and store it in a corn crib which had been built for that purpose. From that we fed our cow and sometimes calf, mule, chickens, hogs, and ourselves. When the ears were still tender, we would eat corn on the cob or kernel corn cut from the cob. Mother would always can kernels for the wintertime eating, and as I was the oldest boy and more trusted with a knife, it was often my job to cut the kernels from the cob. After corn had dried on the cob, we then shelled it not only to feed the animals but ourselves as well. In the early years the corn shelling was done by hand, but later Dad found a used hand cranked sheller which took much of the work out of that task. There were grist mills in the vicinity where Dad always had his corn meal ground to be used for cornbread. He would also have them grind a smaller amount in a courser grain which was cooked as grits at breakfast time. In addition, when Mother had a fire burning under her big metal pot, she sometimes would make a pot full of hominy. Whole grain corn was poured into a pot of boiling water, and lye from ashes or Red Devil lye was poured in the mixture. When the grains boiled to the desired softness, they were ready to be stored for food. Many developed an acquired taste for these corn products, and they became staples to help them survive the winter.

Another crop that we often grew was sorghum cane. Molasses was also a favorite morning meal, being heated slightly with butter stirred in and sopped with a fresh biscuit. After maturity, the cane stalks had to be stripped of their leaves, chopped down, and transported to a sorghum mill. There, it was sent through a crusher to squeeze out the juice. Then it was piped to a large pan, usually made of copper, which was sectioned off allowing the juice to slowly make its way to the spout, gradually cooking until it became syrup. A hot fire stoked by wood burned under the pan to provide the heat necessary to allow the liquid to cook to the right consistency; caution had to be taken not to allow it to burn. At the right time a spigot in the end of the pan was opened, and the finished product was allowed to fill the jars and tin cans that were waiting to be filled. As we did not possess a syrup mill, the owner of the mill kept an agreed upon amount for his payment. In turn, the mill owner was able to sell all that he could get as there was a demand for good sorghum molasses.

When we were in elementary school, we qualified for free lunches, but they did not just give them to the student then. There were jobs which had to be performed in lieu of paying for your lunch. These consisted of cleaning the lunch room after lunchtime and washing dishes. I was given a different job, however. At that time margarine, by law, could not be sold when mixed to look like butter. Margarine came in sealed plastic bags with a red circle in the middle. My job was to take the white vegetable product and mix it with a red coloring dye to give the appearance of being butter. By squeezing the bag and mixing the red center with the white vegetable mixture, there would soon be a butter appearing spread which was then used in the lunch room.

If lunchroom meals were not available to us, we carried our lunch in a brown paper bag. We never had lunch pails. As we never had sliced loaf bread, we would carry biscuits instead. The majority of time there would be a fried egg in the biscuit, but sometimes, especially after hog killing time, we would have a sausage biscuit. It was not the finest of fares, but we did not go hungry

Food was not the only thing to be addressed before the arrival of winter. Adequate clothing and bedding were needed to survive the brutal winters. The house in which I was reared was not completely sealed and certainly not insulated. Cold winds would creep in through every crack and cranny. The only heat was from a fireplace in which a backlog was placed at night and the fire banked so as to rekindle the coals the following morning. There was no heat available in the bedrooms. Quilts were essential to get a good night's sleep and keep you from freezing. In a family of six, there was limited bed space which required two sleeping in one bed. Two older sisters slept in one, the two oldest boys in one, and the two youngest boys in another. This had its advantages and disadvantages. The biggest advantage was the warmth created by two bodies in the bed. The biggest disadvantage was maintaining control of your side of the bed and keeping the covers from being pulled off you. Normally one was so exhausted at bedtime that they slept soundly until aroused the next morning to begin another day.

Mattresses often left much to be desired when it came to comfort. Frequently, when lying down the lumps had to be arranged in such a way to provide the best sleeping conditions. We heard talk of feather mattresses, but there were never enough chickens killed around our house to make even a pillow. Corn shucks were a more likely filling for a mattress than feathers, but I think that it may have been cotton that usually filled the cloth ticking, or "ticks" as the Southerners called them. We did have springs to go over the slats placed between the iron bedsteads on which the mattress was placed. Sometimes those old bed springs could get pretty squeaky during a restless night.

At that time a person was a hostage to the elements. Shade and a dip in water were the best answer to a hot day, and fire and warm clothes were the answer to a cold one. People became accustomed to fighting the elements and survived in the best possible way. It was an unavoidable way of life. Crops had to be grown and the fields tended, and the only way that could be achieved was to get out in the sun and get it done. Cotton had to be picked and corn harvested, and it had to be done in the hot sun. Hay had to be cut and baled, and it had to be done without allowing rain to fall on the bales while they were still in the field. Loading bales of hay onto a wagon and then stacking them in the barn was no easy task considering it was done in the heat of the day. Life for the country boy was not easy, and the comforts were few.

Animals had to be fed, the cow milked, water drawn from the well, fire wood gathered for the morning fires, the eggs collected, and school homework done before bedtime. One of my jobs was to churn the milk and collect and mold the butter. This was a trade-off, as I never learned to milk the cow. There were other chores that I had to do while my sisters were milking the cow.

The cow that we had that I remember most of all was Bessie. She was a very good milk cow, and we depended on her to provide milk and generally had enough. There were times, however, when she was dry because of a pending calf to be born. During this time we bought milk from my mother's aunt who always kept several milk cows and had a good business in milk and butter. We could buy a gallon of sweet milk for sixty cents and a gallon of buttermilk for thirty cents. Butter was thirty cents for a mold. At times we were forced to buy milk when Bessie would get into a patch of bitter weeds which would make the milk undrinkable because of its taste. Dad always tried to maintain a good pasture, but sometimes in drought conditions the grass supply dwindled to the point where she would eat the bitter weeds. When she would deliver a calf, Dad always hoped for a heifer which he could make into a milk cow, but it was almost always a yearling bull. That was not all bad as we would later enjoy a good supply of beef.

One of my favorite dishes was cornbread crumbled up in a goblet with buttermilk or sweet milk depending on which one was available at the time. When one survived off the land, there were times when there was a limited choice on the menu. We always had cornbread and milk which made a good snack for a hungry boy. To this day I still get out one of the old goblets Mother left me and enjoy cornbread and milk. Likewise, a good vegetable plate of green beans, turnip greens with the turnips, corn sliced or on the cob, okra, peas, sliced tomatoes and cucumbers, a banana or hot pepper, cornbread, sweet milk or iced tea, with maybe a big pork chop thrown in will make a country boy's mouth water just thinking about it. I never turn down a big bowl of butter beans, sliced onions and cornbread. A good substitution to this is lima beans, navy beans, black eyed peas or butter peas. Grab a bowl of one of these dishes and add the onions and cornbread with a glass of iced tea and that is all that is needed to feed a hearty appetite.

I will soon have to pause for a while to give me time to wash up for supper (yes, the evening meal is always supper to a country boy even though the more well-placed citizens insist upon calling it dinner, which we have already eaten at noontime). Judi (my wife) informed me that tonight we will be eating collards cooked in chopped ham, ham, and okra, corn on the cob, peas, scalloped potatoes, and cornbread. Iced tea will be the drink. There will be a platter of sliced tomatoes, cucumbers, and banana peppers. Did I marry a good cook—or what? Obviously, I have returned from Romania where the food there left something to be desired to my taste. After forty-seven years of marriage, my wife knows how to stay on my good side by getting me back to eating right again. Maybe I can get a couple more paragraphs in and complete what I want to say about food before I stop to eat.

As we had very limited funds available to purchase food, we grew and preserved as much of it as was possible. There were various items which we had to buy from the store. We grew corn and had it ground into corn mill, but we had to buy flour as Mother made biscuits every morning. Flour was bought in twenty-five pound bags and was not self-rising, so baking powder and soda were sometimes on the grocery list. Mother always used the sifter on the flour and corn mill before baking bread. Salt, (always Morton's in the round container) and sugar were also needed, and Mother and Daddy enjoyed an early morning cup of coffee which was prepared in an old percolator that had the glass bulb on top which showed the coffee as it perked. After we finally got a refrigerator, iced tea became a common beverage. It was always Lipton tea, maybe because it was the only brand that the local store carried. I have never been a coffee drinker, but do enjoy an occasional glass of iced tea. Local brands of coffee, Red Diamond or Royal Cup, were the brands that were used at our house with the occasional purchase of Lausanne with chicory, which was reportedly advertised to make more cups per pound than regular coffee. Alcoholic beverages were never drunk in our house, nor have they been since. Only the staples were bought at the store, with no money to spend on excesses. Water from the well was our most popular beverage, and a drinking gourd was kept at the well so as to get a drink there. Water was carried into the house in a water bucket, and a dipper was always left hanging near the bucket in the kitchen or on the back porch to give easy access to the thirsty person who wanted a drink of water. Everyone drank from the same dipper.

I have no knowledge of my father ever driving to town to shop in any of the larger grocery stores. He made all his purchases at the small store which was located at the intersection of the road on which we lived and where we caught the bus each morning. Many of the purchases were made on credit to be paid when the money came available. I remember that at one point in time Dad started trading with a larger store in a nearby small town which offered him credit, but this did not last too long because on one occasion when he went to pay off his credit bill, the owner added taxes after he had already added taxes at the time of purchase, thus double charging on taxes. As far as I am aware, all of Dad's trading after that was done at the local store where he trusted the owner. Dad did not make a lot of money, and he was very careful while spending what little he had. He could not tolerate a dishonest merchant. The store owner where he traded after he caught the dishonest merchant had a large metal file where he kept the credit tickets. He trusted a lot of people, and a lot of people trusted him as the file was always near full. Dad could be trusted to pay his outstanding debts. Credit purchases gradually became a practice of the past when the big box stores required immediate payments, and the small stores closed their doors being unable to compete with the big retailers.

At times, when the owner of our local store had to be away for a period of time, he would ask Dad to tend the store for him until he returned from his trip. The owner would often give our family overripe bananas and other vegetables. Banana puddings were a family favorite, and with the purchase of a box of vanilla wafers, Mom would have everything needed to make a pudding, as milk and eggs were provided by the farm animals and sugar was always kept in the pantry.

Wait! Hold up on that good cook thing I just said about my wife. She just informed me that she burned the okra. Scratch that off the menu!

Now

Shortly after my marriage in 1970, I inquired of my landlord who was then in her eighties what she thought had been the greatest innovation in her lifetime. She had been a teacher of home economics during a long career, and I thought it would be interesting to get her take on the question. Without hesitation, she first uttered one word—"mattresses." She then explained, "When I was young I had to sleep on a mattress made of corn shucks or whatever they could use to make a mattress. Everybody functions better if they get a good night's sleep, and on some of those old mattresses it was difficult to do. Considering that about a third of every day is spent in bed, a good mattress is needed in order to take full advantage of that time by allowing a person to sleep soundly. Now they make mattresses that are comfortable and allow sound sleep. I think that is the greatest advancement that has been made in my lifetime."

That was not the answer that I expected, but it makes a lot of sense. Today we hardly give second thought to items such as mattresses, as they have become commonplace and are expected to have the desired firmness. I think that this is a good example of how far we have come as a society in the past eighty years to have reached the level of comfort that we now enjoy and expect. Where does one start in trying to evaluate the strides we have made to ease the burdens which were once forced upon us by the elements and need for hard labor? What are the odds that in such a short period of time the world and society, from its first existence, has made such a drastic change? How am I so fortunate that I happened to have been given my allotted time to occupy this land, at a time during which the greatest advancements ever have been made to provide this comfort and ease? How do I show my appreciation for this gift?

The little store from which the groceries were purchased when I was young has long been torn down and the location has grown up in weeds. I think of it when I consider how much times have changed during the passing years. When I go into a large grocery store today, I am struck by the realization that there are certain areas where products such as cereals occupy more space than the entire store had where we got our grocer- ies sixty years ago. The cereal choices then were limited to Kellogg's Corn Flakes, All Bran, or Rice Krispy's, Nabisco's Shredded Wheat (big biscuits), Post Raisin Bran, General Mills Wheaties and Cheerios, and maybe another one or two when in stock. There are dozens of choices now from different brands.

Today an electric heat pump will keep your house at the same temperature year round. We expect the businesses where we shop to be comfortable, and everything is equipped with air conditioning and heaters including vehicles, shops, stores, churches, houses, trucks, buses, tractors, heavy equipment, banks, public buildings and offices, and the list goes on and on.

No longer do women have to slave over hot stoves canning food for the winter. Now almost any grocery store stocks anything a cook could ever want. Many times a can opener is not even required as the lid can be handily popped off by lifting the lid. Want to serve mashed potatoes? Never mind peeling potatoes, merely buy them already prepared and boxed—the guest will never know the difference. This is the case of many prepared dishes which require only the opening of a box. The microwave oven allows one to serve a hot dish in minutes. Craving popcorn? Throw a bag in the microwave and you will be eating it after popping it for two or three minutes. How much further do I need to go to show the advances that have been made to provide comfort and convenience in our everyday life?

CHAPTER TEN

HEALTH/MEDICINE

Then

How many kids today do you think are forced to take castor oil? My Dad said that was the remedy of choice as he was growing up, and he had to endure taking many doses before he learned not to complain about every little ache and pain. He declared that he would not wish that to be given to any kid, thus sparing us from taking it. Perhaps this was the way to silence a child from complaining about how they felt; knowing that another dose of castor oil was in the works if the complaints continued. I am quite sure that would have been the remedy of choice with my mom had not Dad forbidden that a bottle of that enter the house. Mother's solution was not much better. She leaned heavily on mineral oil and Epsom salt. Going to Mother with a complaint normally meant that a dose of Epsom salt dissolved in a glass of water was the key to a cure. Of one thing you could be certain, after a dose or two your bowels would be clean. After giving this some consideration, maybe that was Mother's way of keeping down complaints about every ache and pain. A cut was treated by soaking the affected area in kerosene and applying Vaseline to keep out the dirt.

I can remember only three times when I saw a doctor as I was growing up. In those days doctors made house calls (imagine that now) and on one occasion the doctor came to check me out. I hesitate to say this, but as my parents are both deceased and cannot find this out, I can fess up. I was tired of going to school and decided the answer was to play sick. I complained so much that Dad got in touch with Doctor Jones and had him come to the house. I am quite sure his diagnosis was that I would be well in a day or two. He left some pills (probably placebos in my case) as was the normal practice of doctors at that time (but not necessarily placebos). Leaving a prescription would have been useless as we would never make it to a drugstore, so doctors knew to leave the medicine with the patient. I also remember that if a trip to a doctor's office was necessary you had best get ready to bare your butt because you would get a needle in it before you paid your six dollars for treatment; one dollar of that was to pay for the nurse to give the shot. Now you are probably getting the idea that we are talking about a long time ago.

The second time I saw a doctor was for real. A large boil, as it was called, had formed on my body. I was small and do not remember the exact location, but Dad took me to Doctor Manley and had it lanced. To this day, I have never had anything to hurt so badly. One time when playing hide and seek with my siblings and some neighboring children I stepped on a short pronged garden rake which had been left with the prongs sticking up, and about three prongs penetrated through my foot, but this did not call for a visit to a doctor or emergency room. At first I soaked it for a long time in kerosene and then later in water loaded with Epsom Salt, and this was the cure. It sidelined me, however, and as the school year was ending, and I was unable to walk on the injured foot. I was unable to go to school to get my final report card for the year. This was perhaps a fortunate thing in the long run as my teacher that year was not there the following year. When I told school officials that I had been promoted with honors and they failed to find my record as the departed teacher had failed to turn it in, and I had no report card to show whether I had been promoted or retained to repeat the second grade, they had no choice but to place me in the third grade. If you have not picked up on this already, I am trying to confess that I was no star student in grade school and needed any break that I could get to be promoted to the next grade including running a fork through my foot. As I remember that teacher to be a compassionate person and I tried hard to be her pet student, I like to think that she would have had mercy on me and passed me to the third grade, so I have no regrets that I claimed to have been promoted.

Childhood diseases ran rampant at that time, and when one child became infected it would not be long before entire groups that were exposed would catch it. Common diseases included measles, mumps, chicken pox, whooping cough, cholera, malaria, dysentery, pink eye, hives, and the dreaded polio. The common cold and flu were expected, and coughs and runny noses were a frequent menace. An outbreak of any of these infirmities would trigger a deep cut in school and church attendance.

One of the diseases that had an impact on my early life was leukemia. When I was very young, a girl who rode our school bus was diagnosed with it and soon died. Her parents were some of the wealthiest people along the bus route, and before her death they gave her a birthday party and invited everyone who rode our bus, and perhaps most everyone in school, to attend. No expense was spared realizing that this would be her final birthday party, and it was quite an impressive outing. I had never heard accordion music before that time, but that was one of the ways they entertained the guests. She died shortly after the party. In the back of my mind there was always a fear of contacting leukemia.

Food poisoning was also quite common. I had no idea about the type, salmonella or whatever, but it was just referred to as food poison. Sanitary conditions were not the best at that time and dishes, pots, and pans were not always properly cleaned. With some families water was a scarce commodity, and the water that dishes were washed in was not always changed from one washing to the next. The lack of refrigeration and proper storage practices were often the cause of food poisoning.

Another ailment that was quite common at that time was known as stone bruises. This comes to mind as I suffered from them quite often, and they would put you out of walking condition until they were healed. In the summertime I would go barefoot most of the time, and as a result the bottoms of my feet were subject to bruising and injury. This bruise could develop into a very painful sore. Athlete's foot and jockey itch were often the results of warm weather outdoor activities.

TB was another disease that affected some at that time, and it was very contagious. My uncle contacted TB which caused his death. TB was almost always fatal, and those who were infected were quarantined so as to minimize the spread. I can recall visiting my uncle before his death at a camping site he had set up on the banks of the Warrior River in a secluded area. He lived there until his death, isolated from the outside world. Such was the medical world as I remember it then.

I vividly recall the suffering of my great uncle as he lived his final years with cancer of his mouth and face. We passed his house if we walked the road to catch the school bus, and his moans were heard as we were passing. There were few drugs available to relieve his suffering, and he died a terrible death. I was very young at that time, but the sounds of his suffering. and the sight of his cancer, which had invaded the left side of his head causing him to lose his ear, made a great impression on me. I can still replay the sounds of his suffering and the image of his cancerous head and say a blessing that the advancements in health care have all but made such suffering a thing of the past. His was the first funeral I ever attended, and I still remember a song that was sung there, "When I've Gone the Last Mile of the Way." His last mile was one that did not reach far enough to benefit from the advancements in medicine which are available today.

Dad kept very few medical supplies at the house. Staples included Vicks Vapor Rub, a tin (12, I believe) of St. Joseph's aspirin, X-Lax, Watkins liniment, Carters Little Liver Pills (why?), medical tape, and Vaseline. Home remedies were the order of the day. I remember that at one time Dad tried Hadacol and Geritol which were widely advertised, but they were little more than an alcohol-based, terrible-tasting concoction with little medicinal value.

Now

I inquired of my father, who was born in 1914, what he considered to be the greatest accomplishment in his lifetime. After thinking about the question for a while he replied, "People don't suffer like they once did." Now there has been great progress made in the health field. People do not suffer as they once did, and life expectancy has increased. This has not come without a price as the increased dependency on drugs has become problematic. Substance abuse has negated some of the positives which modern drugs bring to our life, but I think that no one would want to return to the days of old.

With the advancements in the medical field, the majority of the childhood infirmities of my younger years are eradicated. No longer do we have outbreaks of measles, mumps, chicken pox, or any of the other afore mentioned diseases. Polio is no longer a threat. The common cold still is a persistent menace, but there are dozens of products that offer relief. Flu shots are available and recommended for the prevention of that ailment.

With the disappearance of many maladies, others have appeared. As I write this, there was in the news today a story about an outbreak of West Nile Virus in Alabama with dozens affected. I don't recall anything like that when I was a young boy. There are different strains of flu that occasionally appear which have never been seen before. There was a recent Ebola scare which caused great concern. Aids has entered the picture and has had a devastating effect. With the advancement in air travel, there are occasionally those who are infected by diseases not prevalent in this country that enter and cause an outbreak. Thankfully, medical science has been able to rise to the occasion and has made successful inroads in the treatments of these illnesses.

Medical labs are hard at work to find ways to better treat illnesses such as cancer, Parkinson, heart problems, Alzheimer's, and other dreaded diseases. Frequently there will be an announcement that significant progress has been made in isolating a cause and a hope for a cure. Where this will all end in the next eighty years is beyond my imagination.

Organ transplants, open heart surgeries, robotic operations, full body scans, artificial joints, cosmetic surgery, cataract and eye surgery, gender changes, fertility treatment, and embryo transplants to a surrogate mother, and on and on we could go. Will cloning be next? Would anyone dare have a brain transplant? Only time will tell.

Eye glasses have given way to contact lenses or implants that improve our sight. Should it be necessary to wear eyeglasses, only the latest style of designer frames is considered. Older people will become inundated with companies that sell hearing aids. They want to make sure that a person can hear the instruction given by their spouse to complete that chore that was promised to have had been finished weeks ago (on second thought, maybe those hearing aids are not such an advancement after all) without having to make excuses. A hearing aid is an amazing instrument when it comes to eliminating excuses that were made while claiming to be hard of hearing. The placing of a hearing aid into the ear results in better hearing of instruction, and more work getting piled on the plate. This is much to the chagrin of the poor soul who was talked into parting with thousands of dollars in order to have the ability to understand the demands to do certain chores that have been avoided for years.

CHAPTER ELEVEN

CLOTHING

Then

So, am I saying that we kids had to go naked while we were growing up? The good church folks would not have permitted that, so what did they do? We got all their "hand me downs". That is all that I remember wearing at that time. As the church people's children got bigger and outgrew their clothes, they would be bagged up and given to Mom and Dad. Being the oldest of four boys, I would get them first. When I outgrew them, they would be passed to the next and then the next, and by the time the last of us four boys got them they were pretty threadbare. The same process repeated itself with shoes.

Not all my clothes were hand me downs. Mother would occasionally sit at her old Singer peddle sewing machine and make clothing for us children to wear. The cloth in the new article of clothing usually was originally a twenty-five pound flour bag. At that time those bags came in prints especially designed to be reused for clothing. Each of us children took turns picking out the print design that we wanted to have made in our clothes, usually shirts. When we would have enough for an article of clothing, then the next kid got their turn doing the picking. I was wearing a flour sack shirt in my second grade school picture. It was the nicest one I had.

Many of the older farmers wore Liberty overalls, long sleeve shirts, and brogans for their every-day attire. Many had only one or two pairs of overalls, so they could be pretty dirty come wash day. Some had Sunday clothes to wear to church; others just put on a clean pair of overalls to start the week. Those in a social class above us had their Sunday-go-to-meeting clothes with a Sunday pair of spit shined shoes. We had our hand me downs with a pair of well-worn shoes. A few, including the preacher, wore a suit and tie although a tie was not a popular article of clothing with the majority.

The women folk painted a somewhat different picture. They delighted in dressing up in their Sunday-go-to-meeting best. This normally included their finest dress (they never wore pants), best shoes (no high heels), and hats (some quite large). All women wore hats, as it was not considered scriptural for women to enter the church building without the head covered.

I was not an expert in fabrics, but I think that I can safely say that cotton was the fabric of choice in clothing. There was a cotton mill in my home town, and I worked there for a brief period of time before I decided that a job in the cloth room at Indian Head Mills had to have someone working there, but I preferred it to be someone other than me. I had just finished high school, quit my job at the five and dime, and thought that I wanted to help make cotton so people could have some nice clothes. It was about this time that I began to think that going back to school to get a little more education might not be such a bad idea. Not too long after that, the mill closed and the guy who took my place in the cloth room was standing in the unemployment line looking for another job.

A few pairs of corduroy pants were handed down to me, but I never took a liking to them. It was impossible to walk in those things without the legs rubbing together and making a constant rubbing sound, rub-rub-rub with every step. After wearing a pair a couple of times, I handed them down to my brother. I am not aware of just what their fate was. There were other fabrics such as linen, wool, silk, and denim, but I will leave it to the seamstresses to explain further. That is about all that I know about clothes at that time.

In the summer time there was no need for shoes except on Sundays or Wednesday nights, as that was the only time that I would wear shoes regularly. We usually kept one pair of Sunday shoes and sometimes a pair of brogans to use while sawing wood or doing other types of work where it was hazardous to go barefoot. Canvas shoes were worn almost uniquely in sports including track and field and on gym floors. The most popular canvas shoes at that time were the black Converse All-Stars. This was before the Nike age where for a shoe to be wearable it must cost many times what it is worth and last no longer than it takes the companies to introduce the next "must have" version of their product.

Socks were hardly ever worn for the simple fact that socks were not a hand-me-down item and we had none. Neither do I remember wearing underwear until I was a teenager and could buy pairs from money that I made. Underwear was just another item that required frequent washings, and with four boys that would cause more hand washing which would be an additional burden placed on Mother. My two sisters always had their underwear, including slips, as they wore dresses and it was the proper thing to wear. Boys wore pants, but no one would know that there were no underpants beneath them.

Keeping clothes clean and wearable was quite a challenge for Mother. Reliable weather forecasts were not available back then, and if there were we had no means to know what they were. Clothes were washed and hung on a clothesline to dry, and a rain and wind storm could play havoc on the washed clothes. There was an attempt to wash only when the good weather would permit, and sometimes the dirty clothes would pile up during long periods of rain. At other times the wash was made and a storm would prevent the clothes from drying on the line. Reliable weather forecasts would have helped avoid rainy days washes. Most women had pocket aprons that held their clothes pins where they could easily reach them when hanging the clothes on the line. When dried, the school and dress clothes had to be starched and ironed. Most often a person would buy an article of clothing one size too big to allow for shrinkage after it was washed. When men's suits became dirty, it was necessary to send them to be dry-cleaned. Cheap clothes sometime faded in the wash which would affect the other clothes in that wash, and women learned to test a new article of clothing in a separate wash to test the material. If a different color than white or other light material was desired the chosen colors were often dyed into the fabric. Sunday pants were starched and ironed so that the legs would be creased. Wash and wear fabrics, which would have negated the need to iron out wrinkles so that they would be presentable to wear, had not yet appeared on the market.

Now

Today I still don't know a lot about clothes, and I still don't go into clothing stores. I found out a long time ago that some people today have more good clothes than they know what to do with, so they just throw them into the thrift store bin. I never cease to be amazed at what I can find at the thrift store. Remember, I grew up wearing hand-me-downs, and I am not too good to wear them now. Don't get me wrong on this. I am not one of those persons who frequent thrift stores, but when I need an item of clothing or shoes, I head to one of the local thrift stores and am amazed at the choices I have to get what I want. They carry more merchandise than any of the local clothing stores, and most everything can be purchased for less than five bucks. I find the choices to be better than any of my childhood wardrobes. The shirts and pants I just take home, give them a good washing, and am good to go. No one is more the wiser of where those clothes came from; well they are now after they read this. I am fully aware that this will bump my social status down a notch, but hey, I am too old to be worried about things like that.

It is obvious that anything goes in the way of clothing now. Just yesterday I passed a pedestrian who had his pants down to the bottom of his butt. I can only guess that he was showing off his underwear. It is beyond me how they can keep them from falling off, although when I looked in the rearview mirror I noticed he had a firm hold on the zipper section of his pants. Women seem to be satisfied with wearing almost nothing. Maybe that is one reason the cotton mill went under; they lost sales as their product was no longer in demand.

Lawyers and bankers and business executives and politicians and preachers still wear their suits and ties and spit shined shoes because they are important people, and you can take one glance at them and be made aware of that. It also helps if they are carrying a leather brief case, no matter that it might be empty. I suspect that these are the people whose clothing I will later wear when they discard them, as they don't want to be caught in the same clothes too often

Let me digress here and say a little about infants. In my circle the expectant mother will have two or three baby showers, one at church, one at work and one with the family. When I was growing up, it was always a surprise to learn what gender would be making its appearance at birth, but not so now. All baby shower attendees know if the color is to be pink or blue, and they load up on clothing of the appropriate color. After all the gifts have been opened, that child will have more baby clothes than it could wear if changed two or three times a day. The expectant Mother will thank everyone for their gift and comment on how pretty the baby will look while wearing it. The excess clothing will then be given to another baby who already has been the benefactor of two or three baby showers.

Now I don't make it a habit of attending baby showers, but if I did diapers would be my gift of choice. A baby can make short use of a diaper in a heartbeat. Mothers should be extremely thankful for Pampers and Huggies and Luvs and their disposal idea. Diapers when I soiled them as an infant were cloth and required washing and reuse. That fact alone should make me thankful for my loving Mother. This process was repeated six times beginning with her first child. Later, when my youngest sister was born fifteen years after the preceding birth in our family, disposable diapers were appearing on the scene and used along with the cloth ones. By this time, my parents were living in Arkansas and had an automatic washer and dryer. It was not an easy task to keep a baby in clean diapers when there were no automatic washers and dryers. I have vivid recollections of clotheslines filled with white diapers blowing in the wind. They were cleaned in a hot wash pot, then with a scrub board in a tub of water and rinsed. All the water had to be drawn from a well.

Clothing for teenagers today cannot be just off-the-rack brands. If a name or symbol is not displayed in plain sight on the outside of the garment that ups the price three or four times more than it is worth, then that article of clothing is rejected as not being suitable to wear. The same is true with shoes. A perfectly good shoe is rejected if it does not have on it a slash mark or other symbol that shows it to be expensive. On the other hand, it is a fad now to wear pants torn at the knees and in disrepair. Recently when in Romania I observed numerous young girls who were wearing jeans that would have been discarded long before they got in the condition that they were in during my younger years. I would have been tempted to start a fund on their behalf had I not noticed upon looking into store front windows at the mall that those ragged looking jeans were sold in those conditions at a hefty price. If that fad had been in place when I was growing up, I could have made a little spending money supplying the clothing stores with my pants once

I had discarded them as being unwearable. Being a good businessman, I would have given Mother a small percentage of the profits to have her wash (but not iron them because that would affect the price and cause it to be lower) them so as to remove most of the ground in dirt. I could even make a few extra rips in them so as to insure a substantial price tag placed on the garment.

Clothing optional beaches and establishments have also been established in some places. I cannot envision wide acceptance of this, but who can predict what might be in the future. There can be a lot of changes in eighty years.

CHAPTER TWELVE

SPORTS

Then

Sports were basically a non-issue as I was growing up. I never attended or participated in any type of sporting events until I entered high school. I played trombone in the marching band, beginning in my sophomore year, where we performed at football games. Until then I have no recall as to ever having attended even a school sponsored sporting event. Consequently, it is difficult for me to accurately separate the 'then' part from the 'now' part as I write this. There appears to be limited changes in the sports field during my eighty years, however, it has been pointed out to me that sports have made a drastic change during that period of time. These changes have been made possible by mandates whose purposes are to insure that everyone can be involved as a participant. As I reflect back on my earlier years, there were only three sports that I remember as being significant, those being football, baseball, and basketball. I always expected an enterprising, sports-minded person to develop a new sport which would capture enthusiasm as did baseball, basketball, and football. If a person can take a ball, stick, and bases; a ball and a basket, or an egg shaped ball played on a one hundred yard field with strips, why can't somebody come up with something new and exciting? Football was king in the south then, and continues to wear the crown. Both baseball and basketball had a loyal following then, as they do now.

When young, I sided with the football loving crowd as their games were the only ones that I was able to attend. Football in Alabama has always been dominated by the University of Alabama. Auburn comes in second but they have never seemed to be able to gain the upper hand, although there have been years when Auburn has won the bragging rights. I am aware that there are loyal Auburn fans who will take issue with this assessment of their beloved Tigers being in second place, and one cannot question their loyalty. To them, I encourage that they keep rolling that toilet paper as the paper companies can use the business. If Alabama fans can roll their Crimson Tide, Auburn fans should be free to roll their toilet paper until the weight breaks the limbs of those young oak trees. Sadly, for Auburn fans, there has not been as much demand for the toilet paper after an Alabama game as with others, but there is always hope.

There were a number of players from the area in which I grew up who played football at Auburn as well as Alabama. Players such as Lloyd Nix and Morris Salvage were players on an Auburn team that won the National Championship. Others who played there such as David Campbell won All American honors. There are also many names of players that could be mentioned who played at the University of Alabama and were part of championship seasons, such as Brian Diehl who was a punter on Gene Stalling's championship winning team.

High School football has always been a major attraction, with many local schools throughout the years having won State Championships in their classifications. The same can be said about other sports such as baseball and basketball. Winning teams have always been a source of pride to students and alumni.

Baseball has come in second to football during my journey over Fool's Hill. It never appealed to me as a spectator sport because the action was too slow. There have been several baseball players from this area who played minor league ball, but I am not aware of any who made it to the big leagues.

Basketball is a sport that I could never play or enjoy watching it being played. I have never been a fan of basketball. Players, to effectively play the game, are at a great advantage if they are closely related to a tree. Basically, if one cannot grow to a height that allows them to dunk the ball, another sport may be a better choice in which to play. Alabama, unlike Kentucky, Indiana, the Carolinas and some Northern states, has never embraced the game as it has football.

Track was offered as a sport in some schools while others did not. Only a select few sports programs seemed to take an interest in supporting a track and field team. A limited number of students found interest in running and jumping as their everyday activities required them to complete daily chores which left little surplus energy to run and jump in an organized sport. Another limitation by many students was the means to attend practices on a regular basis. Many lived in the country, and their only means of transportation was by school bus. Activities following bus departure time were many times curtailed as the families had no means to provide the necessary transportation. In addition, many students had to get home in time to complete their chores.

With some, professional sports have been a cause to support one team or another, but as there were few cities near enough to create a large following, they have not had as big an impact as in some other areas of the country. I recall listening to the broadcast of the Birmingham Barons baseball team on the radio, and at one time became quite a fan. Quite a few who played there went on to be impact players in the Major Leagues. Atlanta was the nearest city who at that time fielded major professional sports teams, and there were some who were indifferent to anything that Atlanta had to offer as they considered the city to be a competitor with Birmingham in the developments of the two Southern municipalities.

At one time in my young life after graduating from college, but apparently before I topped Fool's Hill, after being encouraged by friends who were in coaching positions, I took the classes to become a football official, calling games. This was between my college days and my married years, and for a period of time I wore a striped shirt on the football field. After marrying, I decided that I would not subject my wife to the profanity that can be showered on officials by fans of a losing team, so I threw down my penalty flags and called it quits. At times when you seemed proud of yourself for calling a pretty decent game, fans would let you know that they were not in agreement.

While I was still on the climb up Fool's Hill, my parents moved to Osceola, Arkansas, where my father began preaching for a congregation in the city. I soon followed. After a couple of years in Osceola, I moved to Searcy, Arkansas, where I spent four enjoyable years as a student of

Harding College. Being not yet over Fool's Hill, in my weakness, I succumbed to pressure and started sooing the Razorbacks. I am making this confession to point out that despite good intentions a person can sometimes succumb to peer-pressure and do strange things. I have since asked for forgiveness, but since I still have friends in Arkansas, I want to insure them that I still love them and wish for their beloved hog a speedy recovery.

While at Harding I took an interest in intramural sports and competed with others members in the intramural program there. Being persistent in entering all available sports and events, I participated all four years and lettered in the last three. I received lettered jackets and sweaters during that time. Having done this, it was perhaps the reason I later thought that I would qualify to officiate the ball games. Apparently, I was mistaken!

Now

In my world of sports, eighty years have not brought about many noticeable changes. But this has been only in my world as I have taken a very narrow perspective of the topic, and many positive differences have happened. A closer observation reveals that sports have had drastic changes during my lifetime, which have impacted all phases of sporting activity. This was brought about by the introduction of Title 9 which opened up a new world for athletics and sports personnel. I was reminded of this when it was pointed out that now those of all ages and genders have the right to participate in organized sports. This has opened up sporting activities which allow participation by females in sports that were not offered when I was in school. Now sports such as volleyball, basketball, softball, gymnastics, track, cross country, wrestling, and others are available for all who want to participate in them.

With all these different type of sports offered, football still reigns. Because it is a physical sport, it continues to be dominated by male athletes. Less demanding sports such as baseball and basketball have players of all ages and genders participating. Some such as volleyball, softball, and gymnastics, now seem to be more popular with female athletes. Track, cross country, and soccer, and other sports attract both genders.

Halftime sports activities are another area in which there have been changes made. Males have joined the girls in cheerleading, and bands now place more emphasis on competition than before. The three years that I was in a high school band, we performed only at halftime games on the football field. I am not aware that in our area there were ever any band competitions; if there were, we were not involved. Now majorette, flag lines, percussion, woodwind, and every other category of sections within a band compete in band competitions.

As previously stated, football has always been the favorite sport in Alabama, and the University of Alabama has always been the dominant team. Auburn still comes in second and occasionally still wins yearly bragging rights. After eighty years, I have had sufficient time to choose a favorite team. So on which side do I fall in my choice of a favorite team? The Razorbacks are out of the picture (I prefer winning teams). I am a Harding Bison fan through and through. My Masters Degree is from Troy, so I pull for the Trojans. I taught for Faulkner University, so I support the Eagles. I attended special course classes at the University of Georgia in Athens, so I can tolerate a Bulldog win. My son-in-law has a mechanical engineering degree from Auburn, and half of my family will yell "War Eagle" until they are hoarse. Some will occasionally leave a little toilet paper in the oaks at Toomer's Corner. I took some summer classes and also some special courses at the University of Alabama in Tuscaloosa. My nephew (brother's son) wore the Big Al costume as The University of Alabama's mascot for three years (the first year at junior varsity events). It should be obvious that I am a very conflicted person so my motto is "let the best team win." During the entire time I was growing up, I never knew of my family taking sides in the football wars. I don't recall that we even listened to football games on the radio, and none were televised at that time. The first televised game that I remember hearing about (a relative was the first to get a TV in our community) was the game where Alabama played Rice and an Alabama player came off the sideline and made the tackle. I did not see the game, but it was the big talk afterwards. I have never been a strong supporter of any college football team, and that is the way it has always been with me. The Alabama and Auburn fans in the family are about equal in number. Since I straddle the goal post and don't come down on one side or the other, I get courted from both sides to join their ranks. The Alabama contingent gives me Alabama shirts, and the Auburn side counteracts by giving me Auburn ones. I thank them for their thoughtful gifts, and the shirts take up space in my closet, unworn (Hint-hint).

My thoughts concerning the status of sports today as compared to my younger years leaves me with a feeling that they are in a rut, and some fresh activities and games would be a welcomed change. But then it occurs to me that the younger generation continues to embrace the established sports which have been popular for generations, and to them it is new and exciting. I have been around a long time, and I am losing interest in a lot of things. At one time I was a water skiing fanatic and told myself that I would never tire of being in the water and skiing. I cannot remember the last time I water skied. There are other things which I enjoyed over the years which are no longer of interest to me. I have to understand that although things get old to me, the younger generations have never experienced the excitement of football, basketball, baseball, and other sports. They are entrenched in our culture, so I think that after eighty more years we will see no appreciable change in the sports scene. There is not a lot more that I could say on this topic as Alabama fans will continue to scream "Roll Tide" until they are hoarse, and the Auburn faithful will do the same yelling "War Eagle". This conduct began long before I came on the scene, and I expect it to continue long after I leave the enjoyment of sports to others.

One field where there has been minimum change is sports. Football was the dominant sport then, and still is. A few rules have changed and safety equipment has improved. Football still claims Friday nights in the fall, and teams still aspire to be champions. Bands still perform at halftime and attendance remains strong. Basketball still has loyal fans and gyms have improved. Baseball is the favorite pastime of some, and softball has given rise to female athletes being able to run the bases. Volleyball has also gained a loyal following and some local schools, as has softball also, have prided themselves in fielding championship teams. Boys wrestling and soccer have also emerged as local sports, and is gaining popularity as well.

CHAPTER THIRTEEN

HOSPITALITY

Then

I grew up listening to the generations before me telling about providing overnight lodging to strangers who were traveling on the primitive roads that passed their houses. Many were also invited to join the family for dinner or supper. Doors were opened, because it was customary that many trips took multiple days to make by horseback, wagons, or walking, and it was understood that they needed a place to eat and spend the night during their journey. The person providing the accommodations could expect the same favor provided when they traveled. Normally there was no charge for the housing and food. This is a clear example of pure extended hospitality.

People were not as hospitable as I grew up, but there was still a good bit of generosity displayed at that time. I occasionally visited a country congregation which was within walking distance of our house where one of the leading members would declare in a loud voice at the end of the service, "Everybody go home with me." He did this at the end of every Sunday morning service, and he was sincere in offering the invitation. Occasionally, someone would accept the offer, and they always sat down to a well-prepared meal that was cooked by his wife. When my brother conducted this man's funeral, he used as his theme "everybody go home with me" as such a Godly man will surely be standing on the right hand and be one of the blessed. He fed the hungry, gave drink to the thirsty, gave clothing to the needy, took in the strangers, and visited the sick. He provided an empty house on his property to a widow and her two children, and he and his wife were foster parents to many children, one of which burned his house to the ground. They rebuilt and took in more foster children. On one occasion he asked my dad to take him and an orphaned child to Tennessee where he had secured for her a place in an orphan's home there. The girl stayed at the home there until her marriage to another resident of the home. Her husband became a well-known evangelist and did mission work in Germany. They in turn adopted a girl who needed a home. I have related this story as it is another true example of hospitality.

We had an occasional visitor who would stay with us for days or weeks. My dad had a cousin who lost his mother when he was young, and he was assisted by an aunt who gave him a temporary place to live. After his aunt moved out of state, he had no anchor anywhere on dry ground so he joined the Merchant Marines and sailed the world. At times when he was on shore leave, he would come to our house to stay until he sailed again. We never knew when he would show up or how long he would stay.

We children would be outside doing chores or playing when he would appear walking down the road toward our house. We would announce his arrival in a loud voice, "Here comes Raleigh!" Dad assured him that he was always welcome at our house, and as he had few places to go while on shore leave, he headed our way. We always enjoyed listening to him tell of his episodes in his worldwide travels and were always thrilled when he made his appearances.

There are many memories of Raleigh that I could never forget. One time he was helping us clear some land when he uncovered a nest of yellow jackets. He had a tear in his clothes and the bees found the opening and displayed their displeasure in being disturbed. Raleigh shed his clothes and voiced his displeasure in loud sailor talk which was not suitable to the ears of the innocent children present. To even the score, he took some kerosene, poured it on the nest, lit a fire and ran. The problem then was that he started a forest fire which took a while to extinguish. On another occasion, he declared that he could ride our mule, Dock. After all, he was a sailor boy, so he climbed on. Everything went well for a little while until Dock decided that he had enough and promptly, unceremoniously removed Raleigh from his backside. Dock was not too impressed with the bravado, tough man sailor talk. Upon the ejection, Raleigh hit a rock, HARD, and he lay there and moaned for a while. I was told that he had occasional flare-ups from the injury for the remainder of his life. Needless to say, Raleigh never again attempted to ride old Dock.

I realize that I am getting into a personal story here about an individual, but I insert it here as an example of hospitality extended to one who was homeless. Dad was not obligated to offer Raleigh a place to stay and food to eat when it was needed. We certainly did not have a spare bedroom or a freezer full of food, but we always had enough to spare if it was needed. There is a good ending to this story which I will share. After Raleigh retired from the Merchant Marines, his aunt and her husband had sold their store in Pickinsville, Alabama, and moved to Arizona to be in a healthier climate. They had kept the house and gave it to him as he had no home. Raleigh lived there for the remainder of his life.

Raleigh was the only person said to have lost his job by the building of the Tennessee-Tombigbee waterway. It happened like this: when Raleigh left the Merchant Marines he stayed on the water but in a far smaller capacity. He operated the ferry that crossed the Tombigbee River at Pickinsville, Alabama, for decades before a bridge was built to span the new waterway, thus putting him out of a job. While he operated it, Raleigh returned the favor which we had earlier extended to him. Ferry service ended at nightfall, and after that he would load us onto the ferry and go to the middle of the river and allow us to fish from it. The Tombigbee River was noted for its good cat fishing, but I remember catching a lot of eels more than anything else.

Raleigh's work on the ferry was not overlooked, and he was given a job at the new Bevill Lock and Dam at Aliceville. There was an old steamboat moored there as an attraction, and Raleigh was hired to give tours and tell people about the river. There was no one who had as much knowledge about the Tombigbee River as did Raleigh. After his death, a local launching area maintained by the state was given the title *Raleigh Ryan Launching Area* in his honor. Raleigh made such an impact on my young life that his name was used in my three published books. It was given to the main character, Raleigh Walker. Hospitality extended often results in it being repaid by appreciative recipients.

As noted in the religious section, visiting revival preachers were always housed in the home or homes of church members. As my father's summers always remained booked up with Gospel Meetings, he was away from the house a good bit of the time. He normally stayed in the same home the entire time he was away for a meeting, but meals were prepared for him in different homes during the week or two the meeting was in session. Other church members would oftentimes be invited to share the meal with the preacher, and it was one of the times each year when the cooks would show off their culinary skills.

Now

This may be a play on words, but I think that today hospitality has been replaced by generosity. I make this assertion because the climate has changed in the benevolent way of helping the needy. Almost no one would offer a stranger a place to spend the night, or even a ride. Some would give a beggar a dollar or two, but would hardly ever invite them to their home, or even a restaurant, to share a meal with them. I realize that if I go to my thesaurus and look up the word '*hospitality*' I will see the word '*generosity*' which I could use as a replacement. In this writing I am using the word *hospitality* in a more personal sense than the word *generosity*.

Let me explain! In the examples I used above, the examples I used to show hospitality directly involved individuals who were always in the picture. Many acts involving generosity are made to unseen and unknown individuals. As a case in point, our church members in a not so large congregation contributed a special offering of over $3,600 to victims of Hurricane Harvey in the Houston, Texas area. The money will be sent to benefit unknown victims of the storm. To really extend hospitality to those victims, we could invite them here and give them accommodations and food until they could recover from the disaster. As I sit and write this, Hurricane Irma has just pounded Florida and is said to be headed this way in Alabama, reaching here tomorrow morning. Church members will probably once again open their billfolds and send another generous donation to the victims there. If there is heavy damage here, there might be some who would be hospitable enough to open their homes to those affected by the storm, but this would be the exception rather than the norm. Money donated to the Red Cross and other charitable organizations would be expected to provide shelters and maybe hotel accommodations while those who are not victims sleep snugly in their two storied houses with two or three empty bedrooms going unused. The residents are generous enough to donate money for relief but not hospitable enough to offer lodging in their houses.

This shift in methods to help the unfortunate can be well understood. Who would hand a complete stranger a thousand dollars and a deposit slip and ask a favor of them to go deposit it in your bank? Hitch-hiking was once an accepted means of transportation, but who now would dare stop and offer a ride to a total stranger? Hitch-hiking is prohibited on the interstate highway systems for good reason. There are too many accounts of good Samaritans giving rides to strangers and then becoming victims. The majority of those who would use their thumbs for transportation only want to catch rides to their destinations, as I did when I was younger, but it is not wise to take the risk. The same is true when it comes to offering accommodations in an expensive, well-maintained house. In the present climate, it is not worth the risk.

There is a local example of this that occurred in the aftermath of Hurricane Katrina in the New Orleans area. A displaced family came to a local church for assistance. As the church owned a building that was once a dwelling, they offered to let them use it until they could find relief back in Louisiana. It did not take long for the church to realize that this act of hospitality was creating a big problem. The family started moving other families in with them and turning the building into an unsightly place. After enough time had elapsed that the families should have found other lodging, they had made no effort to relocate. The church tried to be patient with them, but when it became obvious that the families had no intention of moving, the church found it necessary to have them evicted, but it took a couple or three years for the church to reclaim the building. Their actions also made it more difficult for people of their race (Hispanic) to receive such assistance. There has been no offer of such generous hospitality forthcoming with respect to that building again. Just as there are only a few hitchhikers who cannot be trusted, there are only a few who represent any race who will take advantage of extended hospitality, but it is these few who create an environment of distrust.

There will always be catastrophic storms that will plague our earth (no, I do not expect success in harnessing tornadoes, hurricanes, floods, or ice storms in the next eighty years). There will be victims of those disasters who need help. It is our prayer that compassionate and generous people will always come to the aid of those who are in need of a generous outpouring of love for their fellow man.

CHAPTER FOURTEEN

FAMILIES

Then

I was fortunate to have been born to a close knit family who periodically gathered for events, such as first Sunday in May for the decoration of graves in the cemetery used by our family. Initially we would stay for the 'dinner on the grounds' attended by all, but we soon separated as a family group and gathered at one of the homes where we could better interact with one another. Family members would travel long distances so as not to miss what was an annual gathering. I was never aware of any disharmony among family members, and such gatherings were always the highlights of the year.

Individual families then tended to be much larger than those today. There were a number of reasons for this; the most obvious being that there was no method of birth control. It was inevitable that a sexually active couple would conceive children. This was not all bad because the more children, the more help a family had. From an early age, children were assigned chores, and the more children that could assist in doing work around the house and in the fields, the less that was left for the parents to do. I knew of a number of parents who had ten, twelve, or more children: some in our family, my maternal grandmother included.

Families spent a lot of time together if for no other reason than they did not have transportation to separate themselves. Fathers would leave early in the morning to go to work in the mines, the cotton mill, the brick plant, or one of the other places of employment, and they would return late in the day. There would be only one vehicle in the family, if any. The children were normally left at home to do the jobs which were needed to be done there. There was usually only one driver in the family until the oldest child grew old enough to get a driver's license, but even then if the child did get licensed to drive, there was no car available to be driven. There were very few females in our area that drove at that time. I knew of one man who worked at the brick plant who was not a driver and owned no car, who walked the more than three miles one way to and from work every day for many years. A lot of times he was pushing a loaded wheelbarrow.

At mealtime, the family normally gathered at the table and ate their meals together. At our house there was never anything eaten at mealtime until one of the boys offered a blessing, giving thanks for the food. The dishes were always passed to the right until they had made their rounds. All eight in our family had their customary seating places around the table. Dad always sat at the head of the table while Mother sat in a chair on the right side. The two girls sat next to her while we four boys sat on a bench on the left side. We each had our own plate, which was a metal round pie tin. Mother had taken a sharp instrument and etched our initials in all four directions in the bottom of each plate. I still have that plate from which I ate my meals as I grew up. My initials are still sketched inside, but there has been no food in it for over sixty years.

In our family, two girls came first then four boys. Fifteen years following the birth of the last boy an unexpected darling girl made her appearance after Mother and Daddy had moved to Osceola, Arkansas, when Mom's nest had almost emptied. Blessing comes at unexpected times! Four boys in a row created somewhat of a problem moneywise as we grew up. Unless we looked like our sisters, haircuts were necessary. On Dad's income there was no way he could afford to take four boys to the barber shop every month or two. Mom came to the rescue with a pair of hand operated hair clippers. To begin with, there was no electricity that could have powered electric clippers anyway. On haircut days, Mom would start with the first boy, set him on a stool and start clipping. It did not take too many haircuts before the clippers became dull, but the hair had to be cut anyway. I can still recall the discomfort of getting a haircut. The clippers worked in the same way as did a pair of scissors by squeezing and releasing the handle that operated the blades. I recall the first time Dad took me to a barber shop where I kept looking for the bee that was buzzing in the shop. It took me a while to figure out that the buzz came from the electric clippers which the barber was using.

Fathers were considered to be the head of the family and expected to adequately supply the basic needs. Mothers stayed at home and reared the children. I never knew of any mother who had a working place outside the home except for a few who were employed at the cotton mill. The other work available, coal mining, brick plant, power company, and general labor were considered to be men's jobs.

My Mother was raised in a one parent home, but it was only because her father died when she was seven or eight years old, and her mother never remarried. Grandmother was one of the few working women as she had to provide for the family. She was employed at a grocery store in a nearby town where she worked for many years. Mother had two younger sisters, and they did what they could to assist their mother through difficult years.

Basic needs were met, but the wish list was short when it came to extras. Needs were separated from the wants, and there was very little money left to start crossing out items on the want list. For many families it was more about survival than anything else. Even the giving of gifts at holidays was sparse. Normally, instead of toys at Christmas we would receive a needed garment and a little fruit. I recall one Christmas when we four boys received a basketball as a gift for us all. Somewhere we managed to find an old hoop which we nailed to a utility pole, and we had a new pastime.

As a family, we normally attended church services together. My father, being a preacher, always had to get to his services by auto (or the Studebaker pickup truck), and the family would always pile in the car or bed of the truck and go to the church building. On occasions we would tire of hearing Dad preach, and we would attend the nearby church. It was located near railroad tracks, and we would walk the rails to the road that led to the church building while seeing who could walk the longest distance without falling off. As this soon developed into a competition, we would want to forsake Dad and his preaching and walk the rails to church services. When one eventually was able to walk the entire distance without falling off, there were grounds for bragging rights. It was always fun to engage in good family activities even though we deserted

Mom and Dad in the process. They were always good to allow us children to enjoy that freedom, although they did make periodic checks to make sure we were behaving ourselves in the church services when they were absent.

Now

I think that I can safely assert that the family unit is not as strong now as it was when I was growing up. I believe that I can also make the assertion that the continual demise of the family unit has weakened the fabric of our society. One parent families frequently leave children without proper parental supervision, which breaks down the structure on which needed practices are developed. I maintain that I can safely make this assertion due to the fact that this was my area of employment for over thirty years and in which I earned my Master's degree. I started to work for the State of Alabama in 1965 in Child Welfare and in 1967 in Pardons and Paroles. During this period of time, I have detected the gradual rise in homes where children do not receive the proper supervision due to an absent father. In turn, there has been a rise in the number of juvenile delinquent or youthful offender cases. When I began working for the parole board, we did not have a youthful offender law, but one was later enacted by the legislature. Now it is common for those in their young childhood to be seen roaming the streets at all hours of the night. Children who are allowed to sleep all day and roam the streets at night are not receiving proper supervision. In many cases, the supervising parent does not know, or even care where their child might be. Too often the parents are themselves engaged in harmful activities and leave the children to fend for themselves.

The result of the breakdown of cohesive families has been a crisis in many of the inner-city areas of large cities. Unsupervised children and young adults roam the street with guns, and anyone with whom they encounter and find displeasure is subject to being shot. Drug dealers and users often have a conflict which results in violence. Drug users employ every means possible to get the money needed to maintain their habits. Crime is the preferred method of getting this money. As their bodies lie on the street after being shot to death, the mother comes and wails over it and questions how this could happen to her dear child. To that I have an answer for her: she did not care anything about him/her in the first place, or she would have properly supervised the youngster.

96

All the blame cannot be placed on the mother. The child has an absent father somewhere. In some cases the identity of the father is not even known. With the breakdown of the family unit, he has many times never been in the picture. I want to make it clear here that this breakdown in families is not isolated to one race or class of people. I recently read that over seventy percent of babies born to black mothers are born out of wedlock and this is alarming, but the trend is that this also applies to mothers who choose to bring babies into this world with no family support. It applies to all who fit in this category no matter who they may be. It cannot be denied that the problem is compounded in the inner-cities because of the dense population and lack of suitable employment. Still, the deterioration of family values is the root cause of this turmoil. A man whose main purpose in life is to sleep with as many women as he is allowed to do, and the women who accommodate him in achieving this purpose, serve only to tear down the foundations upon which this nation has been made strong. Men who have no intention of supporting children they bring into the world and leave it for society as a whole to feed, clothe, and educate are detrimental to a strong and prosperous society. Even worse is the society that condones and supports this practice. Failure to change the lifestyles of those who now abuse (and yes, it is abuse in the worst way) the system can only result in further damage to the principles on which this country was founded.

It is easy to point out our weaknesses but much harder to come up with remedies. I think that the answer to these problems is obvious. One only has to go back and determine how this country got its strength in the first place. If it worked then, why can it not continue to work effectively? We need to return to the realization that strength comes through family ties and the need to emphasize the necessity of all taking care of their own. We should not be too eager to give finances to those who take advantage of the welfare system by the continuation of bringing children into this world outside the support of a strong family unit. Promiscuous females should consider the consequences of their immoral way and learn constraint; if not they should practice birth control. There are now many birth control methods which are effective for both male and female. Fathers who bring children into this world should be accountable for their support. There are plenty of methods of birth control that can prevent conception if they are only used. If paternity of the child is denied by a potential father, a DNA test should be required to prove him right or wrong. With the vast bank of DNA samples available now, it should not be too difficult to determine who fathered the child. This individual should then be required to meet the needs of his child.

I consider the generous support payments which are made to some who continue to bear illegitimate children and refuse to work to care for themselves and their children to be a form of enabling. I will be the first to declare that no one in this great country should go hungry or naked. I further realize that the children are victims of circumstances and must receive proper nutrition and adequate clothing. But why should a person give birth to a child with no intention of properly caring for it and expect others to be responsible for its upbringing? To condone and finance this would surely fit the definition of enabling as I was taught in graduate school. To continue to support those who will only continue in their unacceptable conduct is to enable them to carry on in the same path.

In this vein I am reminded of a Bible story which I heard my dad read many times. It is commonly referred to as "The Prodigal Son". The boy got what inheritance was coming to him from his father and left town. It did not take long for him to squander his money, and then a famine gripped the land. He realized that he had to get a job to keep from starving to death, and the one he found was in the fields feeding hogs. The story said that no one gave him anything. In other words, there were no enablers. After having nothing to eat but hog feed, he came to himself and returned to his father's house. I have wondered if he would have headed home should there have been an enabler who came to his rescue and supported him much like the welfare system does today. Another significant lesson that can be learned from this story is that he eventually realized the importance of family.

I am thankful that I was born into a loving family. It is the foundation on which I have lived an enjoyable and productive life. I pray that this blessing which has shaped my life will continue to be passed down through successive generations of my family. The importance of strong families cannot be over emphasized.

CHAPTER FIFTEEN

HABITS

Then

Habits can be both good and bad. My parents tried to instill in me a desire to cultivate good habits and shun bad ones. When young, they placed emphasis on the need to brush my teeth daily. They gave me a toothbrush and the family shared a tube of Colgate toothpaste, and I developed a habit which I still have today. From my second week on earth, I have attended regular church services both on Sunday and at mid-week, and it has always been a weekly habit. I was taught to wash my hands before I ate and to always say a prayer of thanks before eating. I learned to say please and thank you and to put *sir* or *ma'am* after the words *yes* and *no*. I was taught to open the door for women, and to let them enter first. I was also taught good manners, not to gobble down my food or reach across the table but ask that someone please pass the wanted item. I learned to be polite and respectful to others and was taught the Golden Rule. I learned to refrain from picking my nose in public and to not pass gas when others were around. There are many good habits which I learned while I was still young, but this chapter is not about that. It is the bad ones that I will examine at this time. The reason that I focus on the harmful habits is because the biggest changes that I have observed happened on the bad side.

On the climb up Fool's Hill is where most habits are created, both good and bad. As with every teenager, there were temptations to develop bad habits on my climb up the hill. Early teen years are a difficult time to be on the climb as there are new and exciting things to explore, and young inquisitive minds are eager to try new things. It is important at this age to go to the next step above "stay away from fire" or "don't play in the street" to "don't start smoking" or "keep your language clean." From an early age, I was taught to avoid starting habits that could not be easily broken. The best way that this was done was by looking to my parents and others who were setting a good example. In our family it was always, "do as I do" and not "do as I say do." There is no better way to learn than following good leaders.

One of the most common harmful habits was cigarette smoking. They were advertised to be safe and enjoyable, but in reality that was not true. While we were young teenagers, we finally acquired enough money to buy a television. My brother and I made the money by cutting mining timbers with a crosscut saw and loading them and hauling them (Dad did the driving) in the bed of our Studebaker pickup truck. We worked hard because we wanted to have a television set in the house. We were then subjected to numerous programs that were sponsored by tobacco companies. The Marlboro Man put a lot of glamor in smoking, and Marlboro was the brand to buy. It even came in a flip top box. Who at that time could not imitate the "Call for Phillip Morris" (almost everyone then could put a voice to this slogan) or "Walk a Mile for a Camel?" More doctors smoke Camels than any other brand so goes one advertisement, but another found that 20,629 physicians found Luckies to be less irritating. But let us not forget that John Wayne was a Camel smoker. Lucky Strike's motto, "So round, So firm, So fully Packed, and So Easy on the Draw" ended up as the words in a song. Do you remember what LSMFT stands for? You are correct if you said, "Lucky Strike Means Fine Tobacco." Chesterfield seemed to have more celebrity endorsements than any other cigarette brand. Bob Hope gave them his endorsement and so did Ronald Reagan—yes, our president, but this was when he was younger. In one commercial he is shown with a cigarette in his mouth and a stack of cartons of Chesterfields in front of him, and he declares, "I'm sending Chesterfields to all my friends who smoke. That's the merriest Christmas any smoker could have." Arthur Godfrey advertised that Chesterfield was a much milder cigarette, and scientific evidence gathered by a medical specialist examined a group of people from all walks of life, and forty-five percent of them had smoked Chesterfields for over ten years. After ten months the specialist noted no adverse effects on the nose, throat, and sinuses of the group from smoking Chesterfields. Godfrey then declared that Chesterfield was best for you.

But wait! Pall Mall's natural mildness is so good to your taste you should want no other brand. Or with Old Gold you get a treat instead of a treatment. But maybe the best choice is Viceroy because they filter the smoke and the good taste never quits, but then now is, "What a good time for a Kent." Maybe Salem would be the better choice because Salem's softness is friendly to your taste. I think that I will stop here because. as a thirteen year old, I was so confused that it would be as difficult for me to decide on a cigarette brand as it was for me to make a decision in a penny candy store. I sometimes had a penny for candy, but never twenty cents which a pack of cigarettes sold for at that time. Consequently, I have never bought a pack of cigarettes in my life, so a dilemma of having to choose the best brand for me and my health has been averted. How do I know they were twenty cents a pack? They were sold in the small grocery store where I worked occasionally (not the five and dime) and cigarettes were one of the biggest selling items in the store. Camels were the biggest seller followed by Luckie, Winston, Chesterfield, Marlboro, and Pall Mall. Kool and Salem were the top menthol sellers.

This is not to say that I have never smoked a cigarette. I confess that I have—but only one! When I was in the second or third grade, I was walking home from school beside the main road when I spied a cigarette butt that had a lot of tobacco left in it. I picked it up and continued toward the house. I had to pass a neighbor's house in order to get to ours, and a couple of boys were in the yard pitching washers. I asked if they had a match and one was handed to me. I lit the cigarette and sat down in the corner of the house and leaned up against a rain barrel. I was a big shot until my head started swimming and I became sick, really sick! The boys had to carry me home. They must have not told my parents what was wrong with me, as they never brought it up that they knew. That was the first and last time I ever had a desire to smoke.

At that time, it was common to have chain smokers who would practically light one cigarette off the one that had just been smoked. I also observed many times a smoker taking a strike anywhere match, slightly lifting a leg thus stretching his pants, and using friction against the jeans to strike the match to light his cigarette. You could tell a heavy smoker by the yellow nicotine stains on his fingers that held the cigarettes. Some smokers would smoke two or three packs a day. They would almost always have a cigarette in their mouths when you saw them. At twenty cents a pack it was not too expensive for some to afford their habit, but if I was inclined to smoke even the twenty cents would have been a deterrent. I could afford to go into the penny candy store and buy two or three pieces, but the twenty cents was outside my price range. While working at the five and dime, I was paid eleven dollars a week, and I had to stretch that to buy things that I needed. I held this job during the junior and senior years of high school, and I paid all my expenses needed to attend.

Secondhand smoke was everywhere at that time. Smoking was allowed anywhere, even hospitals, and everywhere you could go would subject you to smoke. There would often be a smoker riding in a car with you. Buses and trains allowed smoking, and the interior of the vehicle would be smoke filled. Airlines allowed smoking on their planes. Sheriffs permitted the inmates to smoke in their tight confines. In fact, the sale of cigarettes to the inmates was a profitable business. Public buildings and auditoriums were many times so full of smoke that a non-smoker could hardly breathe. Smoking was permitted in businesses and offices, with the office holder often being a smoker also. Churches were one of the few places where one could go and sit in a smoke free environment. During most Sunday morning church services there was a Bible study, a short break, and then the worship services. Smokers took advantage of the short break and went outside and smoked a cigarette.

At that time a lot of smokers rolled their own cigarettes. They would carry a tin of Prince Albert tobacco and a pack of rolling papers with them. To roll the cigarette, a rolling paper was placed between the thumb and the tip of the weak hand's forefinger creating the slight curve into which the tobacco was poured. The paper was then tightly wrapped around the loose tobacco and the seams were licked letting the saliva make the bond, Loose tobacco would always be sticking out of both ends of the newly rolled cigarette. The excess tobacco on the mouth end would be bitten off and spit out and the tobacco on the fire end would be lit. Some smokers preferred Bugler tobacco which came in a pouch. The afore-mentioned Raleigh was one who rolled his own cigarettes, and I observed the manufacturing of his smoke many times. He could roll a cigarette and have it lit in seconds. He preferred Prince Albert tobacco because it came in a sturdy tin container, but he would sometimes get Bugler and pour it into his Prince Albert tin to make for easier rolling. And yes, Raleigh had nicotine stained fingers as he smoked like a sailor.

Kids in the absence of tobacco would take rabbit tobacco, cross vines, or other substances that they were told could be smoked. I tried smoking a cross vine and rabbit tobacco when everyone present (peer pressure) was trying it, but I soon saw no future in lighting sticks or weeds and puffing on them. I think of the advice I at one time received against smoking, "You are not really smoking. It is the cigarette that is doing the smoking, you are only the sucker." I have known a lot of suckers in my lifetime.

Some men preferred chewing tobacco as opposed to cigarettes. When I was young I would observe men pull a plug of Bull Durham, Days Work, or Beechnut and a knife from their pockets, cut off a chew, put it in their mouths, then chew and spit. Others preferred the loose leaf variety of chewing tobacco such as Red Man, Levi Garrett, and Beechnut. We always called smokeless tobacco, "spit tobacco." The "spitters" would either find a good corner, waste can, or carry a glass or bottle to spit in. When chewing tobacco reached its highest popularity, spittoons were placed in areas to provide a place to spit. It was easier and more sanitary to empty a spittoon than to mop the spit off the floors and corners.

Some men preferred to smoke a pipe, and I can recall that some pipe tobacco had a rather pleasing aroma. There were others who preferred cigars, but I know too little about them to even make a comment about brands. A couple of brands of cigar such as Swisher Sweets, Phillies, Dutch Masters, and White Owls seem to fit into my memory, but as I never consumed them and remember nothing about them from the store, I plead ignorance here. I do know that when I was researching a previous book I was astonished to learn of the extent that cigars were smoked each year for a century before the approximate time of my birth. There were over one hundred million nailed wooden boxes manufactured each year in the United States to hold over one trillion cigars. A Trillion cigars smoked each year for a century; now folks, that is a lot of cigars. I suppose it would be impossible to even imagine the number of cigarettes that were smoked during that time. Suffice it to say, the tobacco industry was a profitable enterprise.

While growing up, I never saw a woman smoke a cigarette. At that time the smoking practice among women was unacceptable. That does not mean, however, that women were not heavy users of tobacco products. Snuff was in wide use among the women of that time. The three brands that I remember were Garrett, Skoal, and Copenhagen. I am sure there were others, but as I was not a user and did not buy the product I have limited knowledge in this area. I know this little tidbit because those are the only brands that we stocked in the small grocery store where I worked part time. The same is true with chewing tobacco. Only those brands most asked for were kept in stock. What I do remember is how the old ladies would sit on their front porch in a rocking chair where they would rock and spit. They always had a rhythm while sitting there. They would rock until they got a mouthful of spit and, without breaking rhythm on the forward rock, put a finger on each side of the mouth and spit. Through a lot of practice, they could propel that wad of spit a long distance, clearing the porch where it would land in the yard below. Often after a long dry period the yard would be covered with expelled snuff.

There is an interesting story that I can insert here as it is one that I will always remember. An elderly lady everyone called Aunt Beulah (she was somebody's aunt but not ours) lived in a house near where we caught the school bus. Aunt Beulah had a high front porch on which she would sit and enjoy her early morning dip of snuff: rock and spit, rock and spit! Many times while waiting on the bus I would sit and talk with her until the arrival of the bus. We would talk about any and everything, and I enjoyed doing it because she could tell some intriguing tales of her childhood. Aunt Beulah was quite old at that time, and she grew up in an entirely different world than the one which was developing into our modern age. One day as we were talking, after taking a long spit which practically emptied the remaining snuff from her mouth, she stopped rocking, got a mouthful of water she had next to her in a quart fruit jar, rinsed her mouth out, propelling the water off the porch onto her used snuff pill, and started back talking to me. She said something like this. "Wheeler, I have been thinking and worrying about something, and I am going to ask you what you think about it. I read in my Bible that Jesus said that it is not something that goes into the mouth that defiles a man, but that which comes out defiles a man

(Matthew 15:11). Now I have been thinking about this and my snuff dipping. I take the snuff and put it in my mouth and then I spit it out. Does that mean that I am sinning when it comes out of my mouth? I sure don't want my snuff dipping to send me to hell, and I can't swallow it. What do you think I should do?" I was in my younger years then and certainly not a Bible scholar, but I attempted to answer her question. "Aunt Beulah, I don't think that Jesus had snuff dippers in mind when he said that, but if it is worrying you maybe you ought to quit." The next morning Aunt Beulah was back on her porch in her rocking chair, rocking and spitting. I suppose she decided that she would take the risk that her spitting would not send her to hell.

I have focused upon smoking as being one of the habits which should be avoided. There are so many more, such as substance abuse and disorderly behavior, that I could not possibly include them all in this writing. The closest place to get alcoholic beverages when I was young was twenty or so miles away in Jefferson County, and with little transportation there was no temptation to start drinking alcohol. I think that I was fortunate that the temptations were not there to entice me to take up many bad habits. Parental guidance, however, has been the key factor that steered me away from harmful practices. We enjoyed watching boxing on Wednesday nights following our return from Bible study. We had no television at that time, and we habitually stopped at the home of our grocer who could afford a television to watch it there as he enjoyed having company while watching the boxing matches. I remember that the two major sponsors of the program were the Gillette Safety Razor Company ("Look Sharp, Feel Sharp, Be Sharp. How are you fixed for blades? Gillette Blue Blades we mean") and Pabst Blue Ribbon Beer ("whata you have, Pabst Blue Ribbon, whata you have, Pabst Blue Ribbon, whata you have, Pabst Blue Ribbon, Pabst Blue Ribbon Beer"). If you are old enough, you can put a tune to those words. Dad was not too high on us kids being able to watch beer commercials. Thankfully, some commercials are not permitted to be aired on radio or television now. The Blue Blades are also now a relic of the past, and Gillette has moved on to sharper and better things.

Now

There are still a lot of smokers out there, but it is much more of an expensive habit now than it was then. Taxes on tobacco products are now much more than the product could be bought for when I was climbing Fool's Hill. Gone are the magazine, newspaper, radio and television ads that appeared to attract young users of tobacco. No longer do tobacco companies promise safe and soothing use of their products. Replacing the ads, there are now warnings on the packages that the product might be hazardous to the health. The 20,629 physicians who once would endorse the smoking of "Luckies" and the specialist who made the claim that Chesterfields created no adverse effects on the nose, throat, and sinuses of smokers would now have their medical licenses examined if they supported that claim. There are far too many smokers who have lived an abbreviated life because they developed a bad habit which they were unable to break until it was too late. Lung cancer and other tobacco related diseases claim many of our loved ones today, because they failed to make it up Fool's Hill without picking up excess baggage that eventually cut short their lives.

Cigarette smoking is not the only cause of tobacco related health problems. It has been shown that second hand smoke such as I had to endure as a youngster can cause problems such as lung cancer and problems with the nose, throat, and sinuses. Baseball players have long had the reputation of being heavy users of smokeless tobacco, such as snuff and chewing tobacco. This has created an epidemic of major proportions in the sports field. Babe Ruth was reported to have suffered from oral cancer as did Brett Butler and Bill Tuttle. Recently, the San Diego Hall of Famer died of oral cancer at age fifty-four. Curt Schillings, now age fifty-one, who was in baseball for thirty years and then did a color commentary for ESPN reported that he suffers from throat cancer which is now in remission. He attributes his oral cancer to the thirty years that he used smokeless tobacco. It is said that thirty-five to forty percent of baseball players use some type of smokeless tobacco.

Marijuana seems to have replaced tobacco as the smoke of choice of those who are now struggling to top Fool's Hill, but are picking up harmful habits along the way. When I started working in probation and parole in 1967, the big issues at that time were moonshining, bootlegging, and transporting the brew. There were those who developed a drinking habit (moonshine) in many areas of our county and moonshining was a lucrative business. Moonshine stills dotted the wooded hills in rural areas in the mid-sixty's. It was also illegal. Normally when the offender was caught, the court system was not prone to throw the book at him but rather place him on probation. That is where I came in. Every moonshiner, bootlegger, and transporter knew my name.

On one occasion, when my dad loaded some of us kids in his fishing boat on the river to fish, he pulled it into the mouth of a slough and we were catching fish (bream) as fast as we could pull them out of the water. After we were there a short time, Dad got out of the boat to go up the stream that fed into the slough to relieve himself. It was not long before he returned and told us to get our fishing lines inside the boat and we left in a hurry. After we were some distance away, he told us that there was a large moonshine operation up the stream which was in the fermenting stage. The mash was getting into the water which emptied into the river and the bream were congregating there and enjoying a feast. We could have stayed there all day and caught a boat load of fish, but Dad wanted to get as far away from there as was possible.

It did not take long for my caseload to change completely. It began when the price of sugar that was needed in the brewing process got so high that it was no longer profitable to take the risk of getting caught and facing a court sentence. The revenuers improved in their detection of stills, and cheap bottled liquor began to replace moonshine as the drink of choice. Many moonshiners also hurt their profession by using battery acid and other contaminants to speed up their fermentation process. After a few deaths as a result of bad moonshine, the drinkers switched to safer intoxicants. In the meantime, the younger generations were picking up new habits which involved marijuana and other drugs. As time passed, more dangerous drugs appeared on the scene, and eventually the moonshiners and bootleggers completely disappeared, and drug dealers and users filled their place.

I remember the first marijuana case I had, as I was not even familiar with it. I asked my secretary how it was spelled and she didn't know. She said that she thought it could be spelled two ways, but she needed to look it up in her dictionary. It did not take long for us to remember the spelling all too well. Following this, there is a long list of drugs which are blocking many climbers from reaching the top of Fool's Hill. Too often, graves had to be dug and another special person buried on the upslope of the hill. One of the first things I did each morning after reaching the office was to check the obituaries in the local paper to see if I had one less probationer or parolee to supervise. I had a practice of cutting out the obituary of a client, or former client, and putting it into his/her file. The probation officer who followed me and assumed my caseload commented on the number of obituaries which the files contained and expressed his appreciation that I had saved them, as he had been ordered to purge files to make room for more. He was able to discard those where he found obituaries.

Substance abuse has become widespread, and it is not just the juveniles who are developing harmful habits. Much too often in this era where doctors prescribe pills for everything and pharmacies are happy to get the business, it is easy to pick up an addicted habit which is not easily broken. Caution must be taken to refrain from that which can eventually enslave one to a habit, which will reduce the quality of one's special life.

CHAPTER SIXTEEN

PETS

Then

Dogs and cats are about the extent of the pets we had at the old home place. Dogs are truly man's best friend, and they were the only animals that we always had, but there were always problems with them. We almost always had dogs that just showed up at our house and decided that it might be a good place to stay. I never recall getting puppies unless a female that we had presented us with a litter. A litter of pups were obviously too many to keep, but it was very difficult to find another owner because there were too many female dogs having puppies to easily find someone who wanted another dog.

I hesitated to include this topic because it contains some of the brightest yet some of the darkest memories that I can drain from my memory bank, and I think that this writing would not be complete without including a mention of my pets. As with most every child, pets can tug at the heart strings and become very close companions. We had one such dog that we dearly loved named Princess. Princess was a loving and loyal dog, but there was one problem, and this is where the dark side begins. Females at that time were not spayed, and she was a very fertile dog who periodically delivered us another litter of several puppies. We had no way to care for that number of mouths to feed, and no one would take them, so Dad did what was a common practice at that time. He would let us keep the pick of the litter (always a male) right after birth, and the last that we would see of the rest of them still sticks in my mind. Dad would put them in a burlap bag, and the last we would see of them was their wiggles inside the bag as he headed toward the creek. We would still be crying when he returned with a wet empty sack, but that was the reality at that time. Even more depressing is the fate of our beloved Princess. Princess was in heat again, and a neighboring male had taken advantage of it and had attached himself to her in the breeding process. After we saw it and had questions, Dad decided that enough was enough. Shortly thereafter, when we had returned from school, Dad loaded us kids into the car and took us for a ride. He did this to get us all together to break the news that Princess was no longer with us. He made no further explanation. We cried for a week, but following that only male dogs were acceptable as our pets.

I know! This is not something that you would like for me to write about as I drain my memory bank, but I do it for a purpose, and this gets into the *Now* part. It is not necessary for this scenario to be repeated today. If you read this and think that this was a cruel thing for my dad to do, you would be absolutely right. But it would be even worse if he allowed dogs to pile up on us to the extent that they would be skin and bones and starve to death as we would not have had the means to feed them all. Spaying the female or giving away puppies that nobody wanted was not an option, so Dad chose what he felt was the best solution to the problem. Cruel? Yes! Necessary? Yes again!

Today, any small animal veterinarian neuters and spays pets on a weekly basis, and pet owners should take advantage of this service. Failure to do so will result in the same dilemma which Dad faced when he did not have that option. I would say that the pet owner who reads this and is dismayed by my dad's solution but fails to correct the same problem with their pets should rethink their actions. Granted, they can pass them on to the humane society or an animal shelter and a home may be found for them, or if there is an excess of animals they may be euthanized by pill or gas, which is the modern way to put them in a tow sack and drown them. At least Dad had the foresight to prevent them from experiencing life and then have it taken away from them, as they would be only a day or two old when Dad would resolve the problem.

Now I will get off my stump and return to the *Then* part of my story. After I told you about Dad and his cruel deeds, one would think that he was a hard person with little compassion, but this would not be true. If a female dog showed up at our house, he would not allow her to stay as he did not want to have to deal with puppies and she was not our dog. He had no way to know whether or not she was a lost family pet or one that had been forsaken. Living at the end of the road as we did, there was no reason for her being there, so he would load her into the car and return her to an area from which she may have come so that she might be reunited with her family. If it was a male and appeared to be a discard, he would feed it and allow it to stay. One such dog remains vivid in my memory. It happened to show up at a time when Raleigh was visiting us while on shore leave. The hound appeared one day at our house in a deplorable condition. It was obvious that he had been forsaken for a while as he was skin and bones and had very little hair on his body as he was covered in mange. Dad fed him some table scraps, and he gobbled them up as though he had not eaten in days. Raleigh took sulfur and burnt motor oil (the remedy then for mange) and saturated him in the mixture. Dad would feed him and Raleigh would treat him every day until he blossomed into a fine looking dog. When he first arrived, Raleigh suggested that we call him Dread because we dreaded to have to bring him back in shape and he was almost (remove the r from the name) dead. Dread became a beloved dog, but we continued to call him dread until he died. I like this story better than the one that I previously related to you.

We always kept two or three dogs of mixed breed as Dad wanted a "watch dog" to announce the arrival of man or animal on the property. They were always fed table scraps. Every morning Mother would make a big pan of biscuits and a big bowl of gravy. As we always had a lot of chickens running free on the property we also had a lot of eggs. Mother would always cook extras which would be fed to the dogs after the meal. They ate what we ate and never went hungry.

We never kept hunting dogs as Dad never hunted. The same could not be said about several neighbors who were avid hunters; consequently, there was not a shortage of dogs in our community. They hunted different animals and had dogs that were trained to hunt for each one. The deer had disappeared from our area, so there was no demand for deer dogs. Usually, they had a rat terrier or terrier or cur type that treed squirrels, a beagle to run rabbits, coon or fox hounds that were used for night hunting. The old redbone, blue tick, and black and tan hounds were the favorite of coon hunters, while the fox hound was the breed used by fox hunters. Coon and fox hunters were very serious about training and hunting their dogs. I was persuaded by a young coon hunter to go with him on a hunt one night. To make a long story short, that was the extent of my coon hunting experience. I still remain convinced that those good people were hard up in finding something to occupy their time.

The only pet other than dogs that we were allowed to have around the house was a cat: only one at a time and always male. Dad would refer to them as mousers, as he wanted one around to keep the rat and mouse population in check. No animal was ever allowed indoors; however, my brother and I devised a way to allow a cat to sleep between us at night. We had a window located under a huge huckleberry tree that opened to the outside. The cat would nestle in a low fork of the tree and after everything got quiet at night we would open it wide enough to allow the cat to hop inside. We then closed the window and the cat would snuggle on the bed between us which added a little warmth in the wintertime. There was a room between our bedroom and Mom and Dad's, and when we put the cat back out of the window early in the morning we were able to keep our little secret.

Now

As I have already said when I got on my stump, things are not the same now as they were then. If there was a veterinarian available to treat animals in our part of the county, I was not aware of it. Now there are a number of competent vets who can neuter and treat any type of pet. There are pet stores and pet departments which do a booming business. Dogs are groomed and cats are pampered, and they are kept inside and considered one of the family. Whereas our dogs got table scraps, now many will eat only the most expensive dog food. Now many cats are so picky that if you don't offer them what they want, they will turn their noses on it.

There are humane societies and animal shelters that now do their best to insure that pets are protected from neglect and abuse. There are programs now available to find homes for those that have been discarded, some extending to Northern states where there are fewer available pets. There are still a few who continue to use hunting dogs, but with the introduction of deer back into this area, deer dogs are now the prominent breed.

Whereas dogs and cats were practically the only pets that were found back then, now if it only has legs (maybe not even legs) and eats food there are people who will have one for a pet. We had cats to control mice and rats then. You can pay a pretty penny to get a rat at a pet store now. We would kill almost any snake that we encountered because we thought that the only good snake was a dead snake. Get out your billfold and be prepared to pay a good price for a snake now as they seem to come in any color and size. Lizards can really empty your billfold if you should want to buy one. There were caged birds then, but they were normally canaries, and their home was in a dark coal mine and they were kept there as a security for the miners. Every day upon entering the mine, the birds would be checked, and if they were still alive and could eat their food the miner knew that the air was safe in which to work. If the canaries were dead, that meant that the air was unfit to breathe, and no mining would be done until it was cleared. Birds today are a popular pet and can live a long life.

Some people raised rabbits then, but they were destined to end up in a pot or pan. Today they are pets. Fish then would be fried to be eaten for the evening meal. Today the frying pan has been replaced by an aquarium, and the tables have turned and we do the feeding to the fish. We raised hogs for ham and bacon. Now they are popular pets. It would be almost impossible for me even to attempt to paint a good picture of the pet world today because the creatures are so varied, and I don't understand it all. Of this I can be sure: it has made a drastic change in eighty years.

CHAPTER SEVENTEEN

CONVENIENCES

Then

What conveniences?

I dig deep into my memory bank to attempt to identify anything that we had then that might be placed in the convenience category as compared to this day and age. I remember that we had a drilled well instead of a dug one, and Dad bought a new Warm Morning heater to replace the potbellied stove, but I am not sure just how much higher this would increase our convenience scale. We still had to draw water unless the well was dry, and then we had to carry it from the branch a quarter mile away, and it had to be carried up hill. The drilled well required a long thin metal bucket that had a lever to pull on top to expel the water. From the time that I could remember after moving from Fayette to Mom's old home place and Dad going away at wartime, we children had to draw the water. The bucket had a small chain attached that allowed it to reach the water in the bottom of the well, and it had to be drawn by two of us kids. After the bucket had filled with water, one of us would reach up as high as we could and pull to raise the bucket. When the first child had the bucket as high as they could get, that put their hands near the ground. The next child would then reach as high as possible and pull. The first child would then release his hold and repeat the process. One would reach up and pull the chain down while the next one was preparing to do the same. Depending on the water level, the depth to the water that was drawn from was around forty feet, so there was not much convenience there. Now people pay big money to buy an exercise machine that repeats the same motions and works the same muscles as we got while drawing water, and we got ours free of charge. So much for modern conveniences!

Needless to say, our small bodies got into good shape while we were still youngsters. There were numerous chores and work that were expected of us that required strength and physical labor. Wood had to be cut (crosscut saw) and then split (ax) and carried inside (back muscles) where it would be burned in a cook stove or fireplace. Working in the garden using a plow and hoe in the boiling sun during most of the daylight hours built stamina. No treadmill or cross country run was needed to build stamina. We would cut pulp timbers or mining timbers (crosscut again), put them on our shoulders, sometimes carrying the logs a great distance, and load them on a truck. I continue to be amazed when I see the advertisements of exercise equipment and their cost and realize how much money we saved by not having to buy any of that stuff, and we probably got a better full body workout. I could never get an arm wrestling opponent because after wrestling two or three, the word got out that I was not the one to challenge for a match. I was plenty physically able to hold my own in any type physical challenge, and I did not spend a penny on exercise equipment. And consider that it was all done while fulfilling a need. About the only convenience and improvement in this field that I can detect is that all this can now be done in air conditioned comfort, and sweat does not necessarily have to come into play as it did back then.

I am truly at a loss as to what I might be able to categorize as a convenience then as compared to those we enjoy today. The irony of this is that if I reversed the time period, those living eighty years before my birth would consider the things that we had to be modern conveniences. The year would have been 1858, and as when I was born, a war was brewing which would be devastating to our country. Within two years, Alabama, along with other Southern states, would secede from the Union, and the Civil War was fought with what now would be considered primitive weapons. Thousands died from wounds which could not be treated at that time. There were many who died because of various illnesses where no treatment was available. Rations were very sparse, and solders often had to fight battles without adequate food to sustain them. There was a constant lack of communications which were vital when in battle. Adequate clothing was always a problem for those fighting battles as shoes and items of clothing were in short supply.

When I slow down and consider the world in which I was born, it is impossible to recognize the advancements that have been made since the Civil War. The Second World War was raging, but the primitive weapons with which the Civil War was fought had long been antiquated and battle ships, heavy weapons, tanks, planes, and other weapons had been developed. Wounds which would have been fatal in the Civil War were frequently successfully treated. Food, although not as tasty as some would desire, was adequate and proper clothing was issued as needed. Illnesses which were devastating during the Civil War and were largely remedied, and drugs had become available to treat pain and fight infections. Radar had been developed, and means of communication had greatly improved.

I include all of the above so I can fast forward from those eighty years prior to my birth and be reminded that maybe we did not have it so bad after all. What I may consider to be a lack of convenience would surely be welcomed and considered to be a big advancement and convenience with those fighting the Civil War. Going back eighty years before I was born, perhaps the drilled well would have been considered to be a convenience as most wells had to be hand dug at that time or water carried from a spring or creek. Whereas we had kerosene (coal oil as it was then called) lamps and lanterns and electrical lights in the cities and towns, if we go back in time eighty years, candles and pine torches were very much in use. Axes sometimes took the place of saws as not everyone had the crosscut. The primitive houses were normally heated by fire places or a potbellied stove and open to the elements. Many were built in the dog trot fashion with the kitchen and bedrooms separated. Being the positive person that I am, I look on the bright side and offer thanks for the things that we had which made my upbringing easier.

Now

I think that absolutely no one would expect me to list all the modern conveniences available to us today, if for no other reason than if I attempted to do so there would be a half dozen new ones coming on market before I could get this thing published. I will attempt to mention only those that made a major impact during my lifetime. I have previously discussed the weapons which were used one hundred sixty and eighty years ago, but now those are antiquated as there has been a constant development of new weapons since that time. Many of the latest weapons have been developed in secret, and the nation has no public knowledge of their existence, as were the stealth planes until after they had flown and been sighted by the public. With drones and laser guided bombs and missiles there has been tremendous advancement in military technology, but if history repeats itself they will soon become obsolete.

But leaving the military and stepping into modern consumer conveniences that made our lives easier at our house, we will begin with the basics. Heading the list would be a washer (a dryer would come later as a clothesline was still in use), a refrigerator (the freezer would also come at a later date), an electric cook stove (Mama kept her wood stove as everything taste better when cooked in a wood stove), and electricity for lights and to run the stove and refrigerator. We bought and laid a water pipe (big black in a long roll), digging with a pick and shovel to provide water to our house which fed from an old existing waterline a half mile on the other side of the hill. The outhouse was never replaced, and there was never a bathroom or toilet in that house. The house was torn down in the late sixties without there ever being an inside bathroom with a toilet. The running water was piped to an outside faucet and inside to the kitchen sink only, but this was a convenience as compared to well water or creek water, and it did not run dry in the summertime when there was little rain.

The ringer washer was a godsend for Mom, as she had to wash clothes for two adults and six children. Children can get clothes plenty dirty, and it is no easy matter to get the dirt, grease, and grime out. Mother made lye soap as needed, because it and octagon soap were all that I remember that she used until Tide came along with their washing powder. I also remember that she liked to use 20 Mule Team Borax and Clorox. Before the electric washing machine, most clothes washing was done outside in pretty weather where a pot of hot boiling water would be available. The clothes were soaked in the pot before putting them in wash tubs to be washed, rinsed, and hung on the clothes line to dry. The dirty ones were washed on a scrub board which was back breaking labor. The shirts and pants were then starched and ironed and ready for wear.

The telephone at our house did not appear until years after some of the other modern conveniences. Telephone lines did not extend to our neck of the woods, and the amount of services available was limited. When we finally did get telephone service, we were on a six-party line which meant that we could only use the phone when the line was clear. The problem with that was that all neighbors with telephones had to use the same party line, and if one was on the line no one else could place or receive a call. We were unfortunate enough to have had several old ladies who loved to talk and snoop and who kept the line tied up hours at a time. There was no way to know if the line was busy besides picking up to see if it was clear. The old ladies who had nothing to do other than sit on their porch and rock and spit snuff now had an alternative. They could talk to anyone else they knew who had phone service. Some even had long cords that allowed them to sit in their rockers, spit snuff, and gossip with a friend. This was truly uptown stuff. The long cord that reached from their telephone receiver to their ear set was sometimes in a long coiled wire that allowed them to rock back and forth without tangling. With six families dependent on the same line, to use a telephone was many times a harrowing experience as the long talkers had no respect for others who might need to make a phone call. Many times if the call was urgent, the only way to get the use of the phone was to request that they hang up so the needed call could be made.

The ring of a party line telephone had to be separated from the other five. This was accomplished by having a different ring for each home. There would be one long, two long or one long and one short, one short, two short or one long and two short. Our ring was two shorts, so we knew that two short rings meant that someone was calling us. If someone called our number and there were any of the party line people on their phone, the caller would get a busy signal even though our phone was not in use. There was another problem here, however. Everyone on the party line could hear the rings and knew when someone was getting a phone call. Some of the old women who needed some fresh gossip material sat by their phones waiting for it to ring. Everyone knew the ring of the others on the party line, so these old women would habitually wait a minute or so after the phone was answered and pick up and listen in. The click when they picked up their phone and the slight change in background sounds clued the called party that someone was listening in. A lot of times my parents would request that the guilty person (they generally knew the identity of the person because of the frequency of their snooping) hang up their phone so they could have a private conversation. The party line system was in place for several years at our house. Not only was the telephone a modern convenience to us who lived secluded at the end of the road, but later the elimination of the party line was a big step in the right direction. Progress had been made since the days that telephone operators sat at the switchboard and received verbally the number that the caller wished to be connected to, but operators were still needed at that time while making long distance calls or assisting in helping rout the call. They also provided directory assistance when an unknown number was needed. The operator could be reached by dialing 0 after which the operator would answer, "Operator: How may I help you?" The standard was a black dial phone which had replaced the old wall phone.

There are things that are in use now that we do not give second thoughts to which were not available to us then. Today, we go through a lot of paper towels which were not available to us at that time. Cloth towels, wash cloths, and dishrags were used to wash, wipe, and dry hands, dishes spills, or whatever needed to be dried. Facial tissue by Kleenex appeared in stores but was one of the many luxury items we could do without. Handkerchiefs were used with a runny nose, or to blow it, and one was normally kept in a hip pocket. All these cloth items required washing which led to more work for Mom on wash day.

I well remember when the Sears and Roebuck catalog was the only wipe we had. By the time all the pages were gone I had practically memorized the pages on which merchandise was located. Mom and Dad always used the pages displaying ladies undergarments and swimwear picturing partially-clothed models first, or maybe they just tore them out and deposited them while still clean down the toilet hole as they had four boys who were too young to be exposed to such nudity. Now is this not parental supervision gone to the extreme, or what? Toilet paper later eliminated that problem. Modern conveniences were on the march!

Garbage pickup today rids us of the trash which is collected through daily usage of can openers to empty cans which are then discarded (except today the can opener is being replaced by pull tops), cartons, empty bottles and jugs, plastic of all sorts, and other throwaway items. That service was unavailable then in the rural areas which necessitated that there be a garbage dump for every household away from the house.

This did not make for sanitary conditions. House flies, bumble bees, yellow jackets, wasps, dirt dobbers, moths, mosquitoes, and other insects were a constant problem, especially in the summer time. Open doors and windows were necessary to allow the house to stay cooler, but then, without screens, it was an open passage way to the inside of the house. Houseflies, many coming from the garbage pile breeding grounds, were a constant menace as were mosquitoes, moths, bees, and other flying insects. Closed doors and windows as a result of air conditioning and insect spray plus the elimination of a garbage pile at every house virtually eliminated this problem.

Environmentally-controlled houses are the order of the day now. Set an automatic thermostat on the desired temperature, and people live in comfort the year round. Electric heat pumps have revolutionized the heating and cooling of businesses, churches, work places, offices, and dwellings in the South, and the majority of buildings now have this equipment. Open windows, potbellied stoves, attic fans, and other climate-related things have been relegated to history but were very much a factor as I was growing up.

The old manual push mowers (muscle powered) were the only way to cut grass then. Then came the powered push mower, followed by the self-propelled powered push mower. The riding lawn mowers came next, and now if you are not manicuring that lawn (it was called a yard when I was little) with a zero-turn mower, you are behind times. To cut weeds, we used a sling blade or sickle. Today, a weed eater will do the trick.

Today, there is no need for anyone to walk fifty yards to get to a mail or newspaper box. Just hop on the golf cart and ride. To walk to the mail box and then follow up by a workout on the treadmill, which, incidentally, shares space in the garage with your golf cart and possibly a fishing boat, while the car sits outside in the elements, may be a little excessive in the daily physical workout department. One must be careful not to overdo it or else a trip to the chiropractor may be necessary before the next scheduled appointment. It costs good money to buy the cart, and it would be a shame to just let it sit in the garage without being used. The same can be said about the treadmill, so to ride the cart to pick up mail and then return and work out on the treadmill after parking the golf cart kills two birds with one stone. Your money has not been spent for no reason.

One cannot get too many of these modern day conveniences!

CHAPTER EIGHTEEN

LEISURE ACTIVITIES

Then

There was little excess time left after all the work was finished that was required to keep up with the things that had to be done around the house. Therefore, most of our family's leisure time was spent in doing something constructive that would make money, not spend it. Vacations and road trips cost money so they were out. Sporting events cost money so they were out also. Sport hunting required a lot of ammunition, so only game hunting to put meat on the table was done. We had very few toys and even less time to play with them if we did. One item we did have was a slingshot. They were simple to make and effective with a little practice. To make one, we would cut a small forked tree to make the stock of the slingshot. We would cut and leave about six inches below the fork and about the same on each fork where we would notch the end of each fork. At that time all the automobile tires had tubes, which on occasion would blow out and therefore be unusable. They could be cut to make perfect rubber bands on which we would attach a piece of leather to make the pad in which we would place a carefully chosen rock. We would stuff our pockets full of rocks and go looking for something to shoot at. We would use old cans for targets and practice until we became quite effective in our aim.

Nighttime in the summer was a special time when we had all our chores completed for the day, and we would go outside with an old quilt for a pallet and lie on the grass and look at the stars. There were usually bats flying to catch insects, and we would toss small pebbles in the air and watch the bats dive for them thinking it to be an insect. We would catch lightning bugs and put them in a quart jar until we thought that we had enough to cast a little light for us to see. That never worked out too well. After a period of time, we would open the jar and watch them fly away. When the June bugs were out, we would catch one and tie a string to its leg and let it fly in circles as we held the string. We were always careful to safely remove the string and release the bug when we tired of watching it fly in circles. It should be apparent by now that it did not take a whole lot to entertain a country boy.

We also learned to use the forest to make noise makers. Cutting a small limb from a young hickory tree at certain times of the year, we would make whistles by taking our knives and ringing the bark in about three inch sections. We would then take the end and scrape the outer bark from the heavier bark and then rotate the limb while lightly tapping it. This loosened the bark from the inner hardwood, and it would slip off. By lightly chewing on the scraped end to soften it, quite a loud sound could be heard when blown. River cane was also used to make whistles. We never mastered the art of making flutes using bamboo as did the Native Americans. We did make primitive flutes from the smaller cane, but we would have been hard pressed to play any recognizable tune from them.

Most of our leisure that we could find time to enjoy had the flavor of the woods and waters, because it was in them that we spent most of our extra time. It was in them that my Native American ancestors lived and found substance to live their lives. I grew up hearing of my great-grandparent's settlement on Cane Creek in our county where they lived. They were Native Americans who had escaped the Trail of Tears and continued to live a life dependent on the things they could glean from nature. This trait was passed down through my grandfather to my Dad who was very much an outdoorsman. In turn, in the autumn we would make forages into the dense forest and dig herbs such as ginseng, golden seal, and star root. Dad always set a trap line during trapping season and was known to be very efficient in catching and marketing fur. He caught mink, muskrats, beaver, coon, fox, skunk, weasels, and an occasional stray dog (which he would always attempt to release with as little hurt as possible). I became quite proficient in finding ginseng and star root and digging the roots. I even set my own trap line for muskrats. I learned to skin the animals and stretch them on boards, but Dad was the one who did this most of the time. It was my job to remove fat from the stretched animal's hide to allow it to cure properly. Dad depended on the income from the herb roots and animal hides to help make ends meet. At that time the hides of mink and muskrats, and especially the herb ginseng, would bring a good price from the buyer.

Commercial fishing was also a way that Dad was able to earn income for the family. He used gill and trammel nets to catch catfish, buffalo, carp, and other non-game fish. He had a local market for his catfish but would make the long trip to Memphis, Tennessee to sell the carp and buffalo, which he would keep on ice to preserve the meat. He had a concoction of oils and scents which he mixed and soaked for a snag line. This line needed no bait because the scent from the line would attract the fish and they would be snagged on it. At that time in the Warrior River, there was what were called Spoon Bill Catfish which were more likely to be caught on the snag lines. Due to the large market for their eggs (caviar) which led to them being harvested almost to the point of extinction, they have all but disappeared from the river.

Dad was the proud owner of an old army tent, which was surplus when the war ended, and he would occasionally load a couple of us boys into his homemade wooden boat, and we would find a good spot where we could pitch the tent on the riverbank, set some trot or snag lines, and build up a cooking fire and camp out. We always had an excess of cow bells at the house, and Dad would take them and attach them to the same limb on which he had tied the end of a trot or snag line. We would sit around the camp until we heard the ring of a cowbell where a fish was shaking the line, and we would jump into the boat and take the fish off the line. In the mornings, we would again run our lines, and we always caught fish. Dad would also occasionally take us with him when he ran his gill and trammel nets. Many of these excursions still remain firmly in my memory bank.

One such excursion I especially remember was one in which Raleigh was with us on one of his visits. On this occasion, we were camping under a large rock shelter which we occasionally used for the night. Camping on this trip were Raleigh, my next younger brother, Dad, and me. I was a young boy with a vivid imagination, and my brother had one to match it, which Raleigh exploited to the fullest as he began to tell scary stories of his world adventures. After vividly relating some of his adventures on the Amazon River (real or fiction?), encountering snakes and other dangerous animals as well as the hostile natives, he had us plenty scared. Shortly afterward, we bedded down to get some sleep. It was a dark night, and as we were dozing off, Raleigh fired a gun which we carried on the trip and simultaneously let out a war whoop. To say that he got our attention would be an understatement. Daddy didn't take too kindly to that little outburst, because I think it scared him too.

Another activity that occupied some of the excess time we had when chores were done was to trap minnows. Dad had quite a good minnow business as he was able to furnish fishermen with bait they needed. On the main road, Dad had a sign during fishing season that advertised minnows at three dozen for one dollar. After having two ponds dug in the bottoms, Dad stocked one of them with shiner and the other with tuffy minnows. He also built minnow traps using screen wire, and with Mother's biscuits as bait he waded the branches near the house setting the traps to catch creek chub minnows. Having a variety of minnows as he did, he had a lot of faithful customers. He built large tile vats in which he kept the caught minnows at the house ready to sell. He involved us kids in this business. I spent a lot of my spare time checking baskets for creek chub minnows, catching minnows in the ponds, and counting out minnows to customers (I always gave them a few extra for good luck).

Another fishing activity we occasionally enjoyed was when Dad would load up the whole family and take us fishing using a cane pole and bobber line. We would always fish at the mouth of Cane Creek or the mouth of Frog Ager Creek, where they empty into the Warrior River at Cordova. Dad always kept river cane poles hanging with weights on the ends to keep them straight. He would have us dig a bucket of red worms which we always used as bait. We would get the proper number of poles needed, stick them through an opened back window of the car with the small ends outside, load us kids up, and take off for the river. There were usually other people fishing at these places, but we would find us an empty spot, throw our lines and bobbers in the water, stick the end of our pole into the creek bank, cradle the pole in a small forked stick, and keep our eyes on the bobber. We fished mainly for bream and almost always left with enough for a good fish meal. There was great excitement when the bobber started to move and a nearby kid would holler, "You're getting a bite!" Eyes were kept not only on one's own cork but on all others within sight. Bottle corks were used for the bobbers.

As I drain my memory bank, I feel compelled to mention a trip that the entire family took to fish at the mouth of Cane Creek. We were very young then, and my youngest brother was still sucking a bottle. Mother had tried to get him to give up the bottle but he was persistent in keeping it. He also wanted to take it with him on the fishing trip. He had his bottle at the edge of the creek bank when he dropped it and it rolled into the water. Mother told him that his bottle had gone to feed the fish, and he would not be getting another one. Following that it was table food for him as he was weaned from the bottle.

Another place where the fishing was always good was at the mouth of Frog Ager Creek. Daddy took us there a couple of times, but it was not a place which was advantageous to catch fish for the purpose of eating them. The reason for this was that a few yards upstream was where the sewer from the town emptied directly into the river. At that time it was common practice to discharge sewage into the nearest waterway with no regard to the contamination of the stream. At the mouth of Frog Ager creek, fish congregated while feeding on the sewage and were easily caught but they were not good for eating purposes according to Dad. Off course he was right, but there were always others there fishing who ate the fish after catching them. Times were hard and fish were fish which provided food for a hungry family. Black women frequented the favorite holes helping to put food on their table.

All manner of garbage, toilet flushings and all, were discharged directly into the water which made the mouth of Frog Ager creek a smelly, undesirable place. There were many reasons why Dad avoided the place, one possibly being his wanting to avoid the questions of why were there white balloons floating in the discharge. He was hardly ready to mix teaching us kids fishing tactics with explaining certain facts of life. A respectable distance above the discharge, at the mouth of Cane Creek, was a better choice of fishing holes. If the practice of the direct discharge of sewage into waterways had been allowed to continue, it would have been a disaster for our environment. I am not in full agreement with some of the views of the environmentalist, but I certainly support clean waterways. This is an area which has made great strides in my lifetime, and I applaud the effort that has been made to clean up our planet. Landfills have also contributed to the cleanup as there are no longer garbage dumps at every rural home place.

I am aware that the emphasis is heavy on fishing when I discuss leisure time activities, but that is what it was. Fishing trips were not only taken with family members, but a group of us neighboring boys often got our fishing lines and headed to an upper part of Cane Creek. We had a favorite fishing hole there which was in a place where the creek hit a bluff area and made a large bend. The water was deeper there than most other places on the creek, and fish congregated (especially catfish) there. On the bank there grew a lot of river cane, so we would cut our poles that we used there and had to carry only our lines and bait with us to the creek. We always carried a big bucket of red worms so as to have enough fish bait. After tying our lines on the fresh cut poles, we would fish tight line which meant that we used only nylon or cotton line, and hook and weight (no bobber) tied to the pole. The bait would lie on the creek bottom until picked up by a fish at which time the pole would start shaking and we knew that we had a fish caught on the hook. We always built up a fire, and with logs placed around the fire pit we would spend a large part of the day and night telling scary stories.

One night we were there in the midst of our story telling when an animal started to howl on the bluff overlooking our camp site. Someone suggested that it was a black panther (which does not live in that area-but we didn't know that), and they are bad to attack people. We took off running toward the main road leaving our fishing lines in the water and our camping stuff and everything to the mercy of the panther. All this was done in the dark after we left the campfire, and it was a dark night. It was a good two miles to the road, and we had to run where there was little trail. At one point on the evacuation I hit a mud hole that I could not see and fell sprawling into it. I jumped right back up, soaking wet, and continued my exit. Childhood imaginations are wonderful things and create many cherished memories!

On another fishing trip there, we were camped out for the night when it came a big thunderstorm. Near the place where we camped was a big hollow oak tree. When I say big I mean BIG. It was by far the biggest hollow tree that I have seen, before or since. The hollow part of the tree was opened on both sides; much like the tunnels cut through the California Redwoods but on a smaller scale that would allow us five boys to climb inside - now that is big! When the wind started to howl and the rain started to fall, we ran and crowded into the tree, but not before we got wet. The wind picked up, and the old tree started creaking, and we then thought it would blow down with us inside. Fortunately, the old giant withstood the storm as it had countless others. Unfortunately, after the wind had subsided the rain continued. One of our group then decided that we would stay dry by staying in the tree and warm up by building a fire. That didn't work! The smoke ran us out of the tree and not only that, the fire worked its way into the rotten root of the tree which was underground, and we could not put it out. After a conference, it was decided that we had no more use for the worms in the bucket as the weather was too bad to fish, so we emptied them and used the bucket to go to the creek to carry water until we had extinguished the fire.

I have to say this! I challenge you to find a better way to create adventure and excitement than what we did. Those were real escapades which I question one could find by playing electronic games, so don't feel sorry for us poor boys who found real outdoor adventures. I recall other such exploits that made the most of the limited leisure time which we had as youngsters.

Such was how I spent my leisure time while I was growing up.

Now

I believe that I can safely assert that people have more leisure time on their hands than I did years ago. The chores that I did are no longer required. Modern conveniences have eased the work load to the point that very little effort is required to wash the clothes and dishes and feed the family. Washers and dryers make quick work of cleaning clothes, and permanent press eliminates wrinkles. Dish washers clean dishes better than the old hand washing method. Microwave ovens allow a meal to be cooked in a matter of minutes. Any number of devices can be purchased to make for cleaner floors, which are better than the old broom straw brooms. Leaf blowers replaced the old brush-brooms, and weed eaters certainly have an advantage over sling blades. The bottom line of this is that there are more opportunities to engage in leisure time activities.

I believe that I can also safely assert that leisure time today is spent in a completely different way than it was when I was young. Living as secluded as we did, I have no idea how the adults spent their leisure

127

time. From my experiences, they had very little time to do anything but work and sleep. I knew of only two golf courses, and both of them were soon turned into lots on which houses were built. Now golfing is a favorite way for adults to spend a leisurely day.

In this age of cell phones and ipads, it is hard to coax teenagers away from their electronic gadgets. Outdoor activities seem to be in the past with many young people. Consequently, the physical activities needed to promote good health have been reduced to a good workout of the fingers and thumbs as they use their electronic apparatus. The result of this has been an increase of overweight children who would benefit from more physical activities.

CHAPTER NINETEEN

COMMUNICATIONS

Then

Communications have always been important. Failure to communicate resulted in an unfinished Tower of Babel. God proclaimed "Come, let us go down and there confuse their language, that they may not understand one another's speech" (Genesis 11:7 NKJV). The value of verbal conversion, one on one, face to face, basically remained unchanged from the days of the Babel Tower until my generation. Changes however, were rapidly transforming the established methods of communication that had endured throughout time. Paul, and others, used letters to communicate to churches in various cities with whom he wished to communicate. When needed, messengers were sent to deliver information and encouragement.

What are vocal cords for anyway? They were given by our creator to enable us to communicate with one another, and that is exactly what we still used them for in the era and location in which I was reared. To correspond at a distance, penny post cards were swapped back and forth through the mail, and letters were written and mailed to family and friends. In the rural communities, word of mouth was the main method of communication. Mother used a shouting method of talking to our nearest neighbors who lived across the hollow from our place. I can still picture her standing near the well and yelling for our neighbor. "Bea!" "Bea!" "Beatrice!" she would shout. Soon Bea would answer with a "yoah!" after which they would carry on their conversation in a half shout so as to be heard. If Beatrice had something to tell Mother, the process would be reversed. I witnessed this many times before the telephone cut the distance between the two so that shouting was no longer necessary. Beatrice was on the same telephone party line as we and communications were made easier for those two. But everyone could not afford or have line access to the telephone system, and there was not as much contact between individuals then as now. Frequently, when someone had a message important enough to merit the time spent, there would be a trip to the house where one could sit down and discuss the matter. Often, these visits would last long after the intended purpose of the trip had been discussed, and a period of socializing followed. If an effort was made to burn the gas and make the trip, it followed that they would not turn around and head back before all the latest news was discussed, especially if the atmosphere was friendly enough to permit it.

Greeting cards were also a favorite means of correspondence. The cards were first the penny card and later two cents, and they often had holiday greetings on one side and the address and message on the other. Many times these messages were saved and stored in trunks and placed in the attic. The same happened in my wife's family, and she has perhaps over a hundred such cards which date back over a century. What strikes me is that this form of communication was deemed important enough to preserve the received cards.

Telephones greatly improved the interactions among people, but they did not come to our area until later in my life. I still remember the excitement we had when we were told that the telephones were coming. I also remember that it took a long time for them to get there after the first report of their coming, and we wondered if we had been given a false report. It did eventually come, but we kids were restricted from using it in our house except for an emergency. We were told that we would only tie up the party line so others would be unable to use it. I suppose also that Mother and Daddy realized with six kids in the house there would be constant fights over telephone use if it was allowed. All these restrictions were meaningless because we did not have any numbers to dial or friends with telephones to call even if we were allowed to use it. Neither did any of our friends, so there was no getting calls that tied up the party line for hours. We never used the Western Electric telegraph or any such means of communication with the exception of the times that Dad had access to it while serving in the military during war time.

Now

Recently while in Romania, I corresponded every day with my wife by e-mail. On previous trips to Russia when I did not have a computer, I bought a card with pre-paid telephone hours so that I could call and talk with her. There are plans available through cell phone companies that enable me to talk to her or text her no matter what part of the world I may be in. Almost instant communication is possible all over this globe. In eighty years, the world has opened to means of communication unheard of when vocal cords were the primary means to relay a message.

Today if you see teenagers you will probably also see cell phones in their hands or to their ears. The same goes for some adults. About half of the drivers you observe will be using a cell phone. Far too many automobile accidents occur because of the distraction due to texting and talking on a cell phone. One should wonder what it is that is so important that the call or text cannot wait until a safer time to communicate in this way. This has become an addiction much like the ones I discussed in the habits category of this writing.

With the passing of years, fewer and fewer letters and cards have found their way inside a post office. The exchange of mailed communication between individuals is almost a thing of the past. The exception may be the sending and receiving of holiday and greeting cards. Today mail boxes are filled with communications of another sort, that being businesses who want to sell their merchandise. It takes only one order from one of these businesses to get on enough mailing lists to keep your postman busy delivering an avalanche of "junk" mail. The same holds true when it comes to e-mail correspondence. Unless people enjoy deleting e-mails, it is recommended that one NEVER share an e-mail address with anyone who is selling something. Now, I do understand that through e-mails one can stay abreast of sales and sometimes discount coupons, and if this is what you want then go for it if you feel that you have sufficient money to fulfill your every whim in shopping this way. I personally, before I knew better, made the mistake of sharing my e-mail address with a seller of women's garments and personal care products when I ordered a coat for my wife. I have had the opportunity since that time to buy all sorts of women's hosiery, bras, panties and other undergarments, coats and dresses, and some unmentionable items at a discount. These are things that I don't even know what many are, or what I could possibly use them for.

Television and radio now have the latest breaking news almost immediately after an occurrence. Cable news will keep people informed of things that that they could care less about, but stations have to find something to talk about in order to fill their time slots. Leading up to an election, there will be poll results announced almost every day to inform you how well your candidate may be doing in an election. No matter that they often turn out to be wrong, they attempt to communicate to you, in a way that might be advantageous to their preferred candidate and inform you that victory is imminent for their side. On Election Day many times a winner will be projected as soon as the polling places close.

Compare this to the days of old: It was days and sometimes weeks before the results of an election could be known. Going back to the pre-Civil War era, knowing who the victor was in a Presidential race was sometimes days in coming. and frequently this was by word of mouth. Many newspapers of that time were weekly publications, and only those living in the towns where they were published had access to them. As there were no radios to spread the news, those farmers and people who lived in rural areas were kept in the dark until they were told verbally about the results.

Fortunately, the means of communication had improved when I was small, but there was still a vacuum between an occurrence and our knowledge of it. As we only had a radio and took no newspapers, Dad would attempt to tune in to national election results after elections. Radio static often interrupted the count at a critical time as it was being reported, and as the West Coast's election time was hours later, the result would not be known on election day for a day or two later.

I never cease to be amazed at the difference in communication in my younger days compared to what is possible now. An occurrence anywhere in the world will be immediately reported, and a person anywhere in the world can be reached and communication ongoing. This is a far cry from the old strong vocal cord method!

CHAPTER TWENTY

MONEY

Then

To begin this topic, I want to introduce you to a word that might or might not be familiar to you. It is the word *shinplaster*. I became familiar with the word as I was doing research for another book which I was writing. *Webster's New Collegiate Dictionary* (I could not find the definition on my computer) defines it as follows: "1: a piece of privately-issued paper currency: *esp.*one poorly secured and depreciated in value. 2: a piece of fractional currency." I bring this up because in the mining camps of rural Alabama the mining operators came very close to having their workers paid in shinplaster. There were many "wagon mines" which were one owner operations, and at times many workers who put in their hard shifts expecting pay received what were basically IOU's or shinplaster which were never honored. The larger mining companies paid in paper script which bore the image of the coal company, or they paid in clacker which also was identified with the issuing coal company. All the major coal companies had commissaries where groceries and chattels were sold. The money issued by the coal companies was not in dollars but clacker or script and could be spent only by buying the inflated priced items sold by the company. Credit was extended to the workers and many became virtual slaves to their employers as they were perpetually behind in their payments, and all of their pay checks went to the companies for payment of due bills.

I am old enough to remember the mining company's commissaries, and I was familiar with clacker which was used for payment of wages. It was not uncommon for someone to have a few clackers in their pocket. The coal companies prospered while the workers struggled to survive. Wages were not high for those who were eventually paid in dollars, and many of the struggles continued for one to make a suitable living. I helped a friend whose father owned a wagon mine occasionally and helped gob rocks (middleman) in vacant places which had already been mined. I did it just to help my friend and did it for no pay. The miners who were filling the coal cars were paid fifty cents a ton to load them. The coal was hauled to waiting train coal cars or was sold for four dollars a ton, five delivered. I helped pick middleman rocks from coal cars and used a shovel to unload coal delivered by the ton on a three-quarter ton pickup truck. All this I did for no payment. Coal could be bought from a nearby brick plant which mined for the clay, and the coal was just leftover, mined to clear the way for the clay and sold for three dollars a ton as it was an inferior grade coal. I say all this to show the difficulties that people had in getting real spending money where they could go to a store and buy the food and merchandise needed.

In my junior and senior years in high school, I was paid eleven dollars a week to work before and after school and on Saturdays, and I was one of the fortunate ones who had a paying job. My dad was paid two hundred dollars monthly by the churches where he preached. He got the fifth Sundays off so that he could go somewhere else to earn a small paycheck. He was continually booked up during the summer months to conduct Gospel meetings, and this provided additional income and helped to pay off the credit debt he had accrued in the winter months. The commercial hunting, trapping, and herb digging also helped to pay the bills. Money was hard to come by.

The winter following my graduation from college in 1965 and a mission trip to Japan and Korea, I secured a job with the state of Alabama in what was then the Department of Pensions and Securities (now Human Resources) with pay of $386.00 monthly. In March of 1967, I began employment with the Alabama Board of Pardons and Paroles making $507.00 monthly. All the people I left in Pension and Securities were envious that I had gotten up to the big money.

The gold standard of money was history in my younger years, but some coins were still minted in silver. Silver dollars were in circulation and could be had in place of the greenback. Half-dollars, quarters, and dimes were minted in silver. Nickels and pennies were not silver, the pennies being copper. When the silver standard was coming to an end, I collected as many silver coins as I could which I still have in my bank safety deposit box along with my important papers. It is comforting to know that I have a little bit of real silver money should it ever be necessary to use it.

While growing up we never received an allowance. Conversely, from a very early age we were required to work and make money. As I have already stated, this was accomplished by cutting pulp and mining timbers. Dad had a contract (verbal) with a mining operator (my friend's dad that I helped in the mine) to provide mining timbers needed to hold up the roof of the mine. At an early age, he had my next younger brother and me pulling a crosscut saw to provide the timbers to fulfill the contract. We also cut pulp wood to sell at the railroad yard. We did all this to help put food on the table, and we were not reluctant to do so. Money to us youngsters was no object as we had no way of spending it if we had it. I do not recall ever having any spending money for myself, except the money made clearing new ground where I was cautioned about Fool's Hill and the salary I earned at the five and dime. When I helped in the local grocery store, I was paid with an RC Cola and a Moon Pie. Spending money in an extravagant manner was not possible for our family as the availability was not there. We never shopped in the big box stores, and there was never an opportunity for us kids to spy something on the store shelf and pitch a tantrum fit in order to get it as I have later seen many youngsters do (one a few days ago at Wal-Mart). We learned the value of a dollar, and that lesson has stayed with me until this day. I should not be considered a tight wad, but I am not wasteful or careless with my spending. I do look for bargains and will buy store brands instead of higher priced brands if the quality is good. When at an all you can eat restaurant, I take only the amount of food I need and leave an empty plate. I further think it shameful the amount of waste that I see in our nation today. Occasionally when I see perfectly good food discarded to the dumpsters, I think of some of the people that I encountered on mission trips in places like Brazil who never have the opportunity to eat so fine a food as what we throw away.

Now

I anticipate that in the not too distant future currency will all but be a thing of the past in this country. Some nations have already ceased using big bills in their money, stating that it is too easy for the counterfeiters to duplicate. Plastic is rapidly taking the place of spending money as more and more people pay with their credit and debit cards. It is more convenient just to swipe or insert a card than it is to fool with bills and change.

Most payments now are handled directly by the banks, and very little currency changes hands now. Direct deposits and direct withdrawals eliminate the hassle of receiving and depositing pay checks, and loan and other payments can be automatically deducted from a bank account. Charitable contributions are normally made by check, not cash, in order to keep a record for income tax purposes. Gift cards are often given in the place of money, and these are often purchased by plastic.

Unlike my younger years, many youngsters expect a healthy allowance to go on top of their demand for designer clothes and shoes. Any work performed around the house such as cutting grass comes with a demand for payment. Also expected is the latest in electronic gadgetry to be bought for their leisure time entertainment. Clothing and shoes must meet the standard of extravagance or else! Money comes easy for them as their parents rush to fill their every wish.

Salaries now are sometimes so high that the ones that were paid eighty years ago would not cover the money that is now spent for coffee breaks. Automation and robots have virtually eliminated the need for strong physical labor in the factories. There are those who must still battle the elements such as construction workers, but these jobs have been made easier by the use of heavy equipment, some offering air conditioned comfort while being operated. Farmers have air conditioned cabs on their tractors and the latest state-of-the arts controls to simplify operations.

That which I write today is common knowledge and the reader may question why I even bother to mention these things, but in writing this I am also looking ahead eighty years and wonder what one who might be reading this then may think. Going back in time eighty years as I have done demonstrates that a drastic change can occur in that period of time. Fast forward eighty years and try to visualize what changes may occur between now and then in regard to money and the methods of paying for merchandise and due bills. Only time will tell.

CHAPTER TWENTY-ONE

OFFICES

Then

I knew very little about offices as I was growing up. Well, that is not exactly the truth. I made quite a few trips to the principal's office at the instructions of my teachers, but I think that has no bearing on the subject at hand. About the only thing that I knew then that was kept in the principal's office was the board of education, and this board is not required to be capitalized. Most of the time it was not used on me, but it was displayed to enforce the threat that it could be brought into play should the misbehavior continue. And yes, this was not an empty threat as the paddle was used if the teacher or principal thought it was justified. I don't remember ever having been paddled, but the threat was enough to straighten me out. I did witness it in use many times, and this was deterrent enough for me; I was not exactly a slow learner.

Office supplies and equipment at that time were primitive as compared to today. My dad had an office in the church building where he published a church bulletin each week. The only typewriter that was available was a Royal manual that required the carriage to be returned manually with each line. To print the bulletin required a mimeograph machine, where ink had to be spread on the drum and the copy was initially stamped out letters that allowed the ink to seep through to print the paper sheets as they were manually cranked through the machine. It was often a messy job as just the right amount of ink was needed to do a neat job. If additional copies were needed, a sheet or sheets of carbon paper were used. These were inserted under the original to allow the carbon from the paper to make additional copies. Mistakes were difficult to correct as a typing eraser was used, and if carbon paper was being used each sheet required erasing as to erase only the top mistake resulted in the carbon paper smearing those underneath. In Dad's office, an old wooden straight chair served as the seating while typing or writing.

If one was fortunate enough to have a secretary, dictation had to be taken in shorthand. There was no recording equipment available for verbal dictations in any office that I was aware of around where we were raised, and I am not sure that there were any obtainable at that time. In hiring a secretary, the number of words and the efficiency of shorthand that the person could do was often the determining factor for the hire.

Going a very long way back in time, about the only handwriting instrument was a lead pencil, most often in yellow. When ink was used, I recall the old bladder type fountain pens that had a lever on the side to draw the ink from the bottle into the bladder. The writing tip was metal with a tiny slit in the middle. In school, some desks had a round cup hole set in the desk to accommodate the ink jar which had a small upper cup to catch enough ink to fill the pen. This allowed the filling of the pen without having to dip the pen deep into the bottle which would prevent the use of the side lever. In the office, the ink jar was normally kept in an upper drawer under the desk. I recall when the ball point pens first hit the market that they were not cheap, but they were a huge advancement over the ink pen. It did not take long, however, before the fountain pen and ink bottle were relegated to history. No longer would school children return from school having spilled ink on their finest school clothes.

In the office, letters had to be written and mailed. This required envelopes where the stamps had to be licked or moistened in order to affix them to the envelope. Incoming mail had to be opened and read, and many times a response was necessary which required the use of the manual typewriter. Daily bank deposits were many times necessary.

Office lighting many times was poor. The desk lamp made its appearance and sat on many desks in order to provide adequate lighting. Many offices were hot and stuffy, and a fan was used to circulate the air. Caution had to be taken to place the fan where it would not blow papers around that were stacked on nearby desks. The breeze could play havoc on an organized desk by blowing papers onto the floor and all sequenced order was then lost. With the coming of electricity in the small towns where I lived, the work in an office was improved greatly with the replacement of kerosene light and the use of fans to make the tight enclosure more comfortable. It would be later when electric office equipment such as typewriters and copy machines and air conditioning would even further relieve the work load.

I started to work in an office setting in 1965 when I began my employment with the state of Alabama. At first, all my dictation was taken in shorthand by my secretary who had just graduated to the use of an electric Underwood typewriter over the use of a manual one. Doing house calls and investigations, there was no means of communication outside the office. When I started doing work in the courts, the court reporter recorded the proceedings by shorthand, soon after to be aided by a recording machine. The manual necessity to transcribe the testimony taken in the courtroom was because often times the judge or one of the attorneys would request that certain testimony be read back, and the court reporter had to rely on the accuracy of her (always female in our courtroom) shorthand to comply with the request. I relied heavily on secretaries to do the required office work and was fortunate to have had some of the best. Many of the forms were made into duplicates where multiple copies could be made at one typing. The problem of this was the necessity of correcting them all should a mistake be made. Xerox solved this problem but not until the later years of my employment with the state as I am nearing the eighteenth year of my retirement, and the state was slow in getting us a copy machine. They probably wanted to get rid of all their preprinted duplicate forms before they invested in copy machines and the additional paper and ink that were required in using one. There was ALWAYS a shortage of funds to adequately supply the local offices, although they never seemed to have this problem in the central office in Montgomery. In our office the word processors, computers, copy machines, and other outside forms of communication were to come at a later date.

Now

The office conditions as described above are now a distant memory. Gradually the old Royal or Underwood manual typewriters gave way to electric ones whose strikers morphed into balls covered by the alphabet. This in turn was replaced by word processers, then primitive computers which developed to the point that they now make automatic corrections and notify the user when an error is detected. Computers now furnish a dictionary and thesaurus and then allow the message to be sent almost instantly. Almost gone are the days when letters had to be mailed and stamps affixed. There is little incoming mail that necessitates letters being opened and placed on the proper desk for reply. The magic of electronics allows the flow of communications directly between interested parties and simplifies interaction among them. Snail mail is slowly crawling to an end and being replaced by correspondence sent by modern innovations. Almost all banking is done electronically, thus eliminating frequent trips to the bank. Pay checks are deposited electronically and payments are made in the same way. Direct deposits and direct withdrawals are set up so that the worry is taken out of being on time with the payments.

All this is done in air conditioned comfort while sitting in an adjustable, soft, easy chair. No longer is a secretary required to take dictation in shorthand; electronics have replaced that necessity. Computers and calculators take much of the work out of accounting and bookkeeping and often are more mistake-proof. Communications have been modernized to allow automatic answering to aid a person in directing a call and having a question answered, rather than speaking to an individual. When one follows instructions and enters the correct numbers, the inquiry will be answered automatically without the aid of an individual.

Gone are the carbon papers and typing erasers. No longer are trips necessary to the printer for the making of copies. Xerox appeared on the scene and copy machines have become standard office equipment. It is hard to imagine how an office could function properly now without a copy machine. When first introduced, a specialized paper was required, but now standard paper fills the bill.

When pictures are required, the digitalized camera and memory sticks allow the making and storing of pictures to be a simple process. The camera no longer requires film to be sent off to be developed and is easy to operate. Whereas once camera adjustments were required to get a clear photograph, now one has only to point and shoot. Flash drives also come to the rescue in the transfer and storage of pictures and documents from a computer. I suspect that in eighty years one who might be reading this will get a good laugh at the archaic methods that we now call modern advancements. They may probably have no clue about what I mention in our having memory cards and flash drives just as many today are not familiar with floppy disks, VHS tapes, and other items that appeared and soon disappeared in the not too distant past. Time marches on and with it constant changes. What is the rave today will soon be antiquated and there will be a replacement—and the cycle will continue.

Will secretaries be necessary after the passing of eighty more years, or might they be more in demand to keep up with advancements that are made? Will electronics advance to the point where the duties that are now done in an office setting will be automatically done in the same way that communication advances have impacted the way information is dispersed and inquiries are now answered. You can be assured that today there are those who are working to simplify the work that is now done in an office setting. Tomorrow, new time saving "gadgets" and equipment will appear.

CHAPTER TWENTY-TWO

DEATHS/FUNERALS

Then

You shall surely die! This is a topic we always have in the back of our minds, yet we want to bring it to the forefront only when it stares us in the face. This is one thing that has not changed since the beginning of mankind and will always be. So why would I choose this as a topic to discuss? It is not death that strikes me as being different, but life as it leads to that death and the method of dealing with the deceased after death.

First, I look into the mirror today and see an old man. When I was young, I would have thought a person my age to be old and near death, and this could very well have been the case with me, yet life expectancy today is much longer than it was eighty years ago. Yes. I am an old man, but I plan to continue to enjoy every day that I have left to live. I have reached the age when the majority of obituaries in the daily paper give an age of the deceased to be younger than I am. I attribute this largely to the decisions which I made on the climb up Fools Hill to take care of my special body and avoid harmful habits and activities. I was truly fortunate that I had the parental supervision that I had and a good example to follow. I often wonder if those who die much younger than what I now am had a more difficult climb up the hill and would have had a longer life if earlier in that life they had been guided through the pitfalls created by harmful habits.

I say this realizing that many are the victims of unavoidable diseases caused by a weakness of their body, inherited diseases, or environmental conditions. I have had far too many friends, however, who died at a relatively early age of lung cancer, cirrhosis of the liver, or other diseases which their doctors attributed to tobacco smoking, alcohol, or other harmful substances. Many productive lives have been cut short due to mistakes made early in life.

Throughout the years our family has been very fortunate to have a record of longevity. There is always the exception, and the loss of a family member leaves a great void in our lives. The first death and funeral which I recall in my formative years was that of a great uncle who lived in the last house before reaching our house where the road ended. It was necessary to pass his house in order to reach ours. He had cancer of the mouth and throat which I attribute to his use of snuff tobacco. I still remember how horrifying it was when I would pass his house and he would be on the porch with the cancer having eaten out the side of his face and ear. He kept gauze and tape on it, but the wound would release matter that had to be cleaned from the side of his face. After his death, I attended his funeral and still remember those having the congregation sing "The Last Mile of the Way" during the service. It made quite an impression on me as they lowered him into the grave as I was told that he would no longer be living as our neighbor.

It was common procedure then for the body to be returned and viewed at the house of the deceased, many times without being embalmed or a funeral home involved in the burial. There were some who made their own wooden coffins to be used for their burial, so there was no need for a funeral home to become involved. It was not until later that restrictions were placed on a human burial. I can recall there being talk of the need to quickly bury a body after death before the body became discolored and foul smelling. Bodies were normally dressed in their best Sunday clothes, but sometimes men were buried in their best pair of overalls. They would lie in state throughout a night or two before the funeral. There would be those who kept a round-the-clock vigilance over the body with someone with a hand fan or cloth keeping the flies away from the corpse. As the house windows and doors were opened to provide the circulation of air, this also allowed entrance to flies and bugs. I recall that there would be some who would stand over the body and wail for a long period of time.

Funerals were normally conducted in a church building where the family cemetery was located. When the time came to move the body, depending on the popularity of the deceased as to the length it would be, a funeral procession would form, and with headlights on, proceed to the place where the funeral would be held. If a funeral home was involved, leading the procession would be a law enforcement car with lights flashing. If coming out of town, there would be law officers rushing to block all intersections so as not to allow cars to break up the procession. The cars in the procession could be identified by having their head lights on. All oncoming traffic would stop in respect for the deceased and continue only after all cars in the procession had passed. The preacher who would conduct the funeral would follow the police escort which was then followed by the hearse carrying the body. Following the hearse would be the car, or cars which transported the immediate family. Other family members and friends would then make up the remainder of the procession. A very prominent or popular person would frequently have a long line of cars following in the procession.

In the church building before the final closing of the casket, there would often be family members who would stand in front of the casket and sob as they viewed the body. It was not uncommon for one or more to collapse and have to be helped to a bench to recover. For this reason a strong relative or friend would keep guard on the casket to catch anyone who might fall in order to prevent an injury.

When there was a grave to be dug and then filled to cover the casket, men of the community would take turns using the pick and shovel. All graves had to be hand dug and six feet deep as there were no vaults then. The casket would rest in a wooden box. The depth was important as the wooden box would rot away after a few years, and the grave would sink slightly. There was enough dirt needed to fill in the grave when this occurred so as not to expose the casket. For this reason enough dirt was left above the gravesite to form an inverted V shape to accommodate for later need. The modern vault today eliminates that problem, and no longer does the depth of the grave require neither the six feet nor does there need to be excess dirt left over the gravesite.

After the funeral services, the pall bearers would carry the casket to the open grave where there would be a graveside service with chairs provided for the family. The weeping at this time would sometimes reach its height and after a Bible reading (the 23rd Psalm more often than not) and a prayer, the preacher conducting the funeral would go to each family member and say words of comfort. It was then time to lower the body into the grave where those with shovels would close the grave and leave enough dirt on top to heap it into that inverted V which was firmly packed to allow flowers (real—not artificial) to be placed on the grave.

Now

Today your demise can set survivors back a pretty penny. Granted, it is not cheap to live, but it is not cheap to die either. No longer are there craftsmen constructing wooden boxes for the final resting places; the Amish may be an exception. The more luxurious your final bed, the more it will cost you. It will be lowered into an expensive vault and closed, only then to have dirt thrown on it: that is, unless loved ones choose to spend a lot more money and place your body in a crypt. Now, I am saying all this to get around to the point that it ain't what it used to be. The whole dying and getting buried process seems to have changed completely since I was a toddler. Recently while hiking in the Bankhead forest, I came across an old cemetery with a few tombstones, but mostly stones as grave markers. What caught my eye was a tombstone that had the date of death to have been the day before I was born. I surmise that with the earlier burials like they had then, that on the Sunday afternoon that I was born they were laying her in her grave. Generations come and generations go, and when it comes your turn to inhabit this earth a wise person will make the most out of life as is possible. This is why I have said from the beginning of my writings here that we are all born privileged; therefore, every life is sacred no matter what race, color, gender or social status we may be.

So it is certain that we will all leave this world in the same way we entered. Death is certain, and we will carry nothing with us into eternity. We then turn the duties over to the next generation for them to plot the future. The blueprints that we have set before them will be their guide as life on earth continues. If this blueprint is clear with practical plans for the climb that the young must take up Fool's Hill and a successful descent made, this nation will be in good hands. History teaches that the rot from within a nation will cause it to collapse. We pray that future generations will be diligent to ensure that our nation continues in the future to build upon the strong foundation on which the United States of America was founded.

You are completely right! I got back on my soapbox again proclaiming a message about the security of our nation when I am supposed to be discussing the topic of death and funerals. I can attribute this to my great concern for my children, grandchildren, and their descendants who will inherit our family's limited share of earth and time. When the lid of the coffin is closed on me for the last time, any future input that I may have had will be covered with sod.

So what about my view of this topic today and how has it changed since my first remembrances? The old has given way to the new and there is very little resemblance between the two. I can remember my mother and father cautioning me not to put half dollar coins in my mouth saying that they may have been used to place over a dead man's eyes in order that they be closed as people sometimes died with their eyes open, and the coins would insure that they be closed as the body stiffened in death. They had supposedly witnessed this, but I am not too convinced of that, although it may have been a standard practice at that time. I can say this, assuredly, that practice has long been abandoned as have the half dollar coins. Bodies are immediately transported to a funeral home where they are prepared for a proper burial. Whereas eighty years ago it seems to me that the majority of deaths occurred at a person's home in his bed, today most, but not all, bodies are picked up at hospitals and nursing homes where they spent their final hours.

With the exception of dignitaries, the funeral procession is all but history. No longer will law enforcement take the time to lead a procession, nor will cars stop to honor the deceased. Whereas once an enclosed funeral and a graveside service were a common practice, more and more families forgo the funeral and have only a graveside service or no service at all. Now most funerals are conducted in funeral homes as opposed to church buildings which was the standard practice in the thirties and forties. It is getting to be customary now to forgo a graveside service following a funeral, and family and friends will go to the gravesite only after the grave is closed and the flowers placed on it. On the subject of flowers, I can recall funerals where the amount of flowers could hardly fit in the church house where most funerals were conducted. They would cover the front and line the walls to the rear of the church. Over time there has been a shift as people begin to realize that the excessive amount of flowers that would only wither and die if fresh, or clutter the cemetery if artificial, benefitted the flower shops more than anyone else. A gift to a church or a favorite charity serves the same purpose for showing sympathy and serves more of a useful purpose.

One thing that has really struck me as having changed is the atmosphere at deaths and funerals. With the exception of tragic, unexpected deaths, there is not the emotion shown as in my first remembrances. It seems that today when people gather for wakes and funerals there is more laughter than tears. The wailing, sobbing, and fainting seems to have eased into history. I think that it is not a lack of love for the deceased and family, but the realization that death is inevitable, and the person has reached their final destination.

More and more people are choosing to be cremated. This was unheard of in the society in which I was raised. Funeral expenses have become so high that it is far less expensive to have the body cremated. The expenses of funeral homes in preparing the bodies and conducting funerals, plus an expensive burial plot are thus eliminated. A memorial service can then be held without the body present, and thus the memory of the deceased be honored in this fashion.

CHAPTER TWENTY-THREE

HOLIDAYS

Holidays in our family were not much different than any other day. A day off from one activity only led to another one of work in a different place. When I consider that we had practically the same holidays then as now, I find it hard to even place a connection to a specific holiday and the ways our family celebrated them. As another disclaimer, I had to pick the brains of some of my siblings at that time to serve as a reminder of anything that was special about any holiday. I basically hit a blank with all but an older sister who recalled a few things that she considered special at holiday time.

Christmas

Then

While growing up, we expected little for Christmas, and our expectations were usually met. We were never led to believe that there was a Santa and, therefore, never expected him to come down our chimney. Mother let us know from the get-go that Dad was the Santa, and he didn't have the money to spend on gifts. The only gift that I remember receiving on Christmas Day was a shared basketball for me and my next oldest brother as we always shared a gift. My two older sisters shared a gift as did my two younger brothers. Mainly at Christmas we had apples saved from our trees and a candy cane. The fun of Christmastime, was not in the receiving of gifts but in the preparation for the day. It all started after the school's dismissal for Christmas and New Year's when we had a little extra time on our hands. The community kids as a group would all gather at our house for a Christmas tree hunt. As we had the most property of anyone else around, we would take off looking for the perfect tree. This was a challenge as we always used red cedar trees, and even though they were plentiful in other areas of the county, they were hard to find on our property, or surrounding property for that matter, and it was even harder to find the perfect tree.

This would inevitably turn into more of an excursion than a search. I remember that one year we had ventured onto surrounding property, which belonged to out-of-towners, since we had no success in finding the right trees on our property. This was very hilly terrain, and we came across a very large bolder about the size of a VW Rabbit and decided that we would roll that thing off the hill. We found a good-sized, round pole and rolled a rock next to the larger one to be used as a fulcrum for the pole. There were a number of us in the group, and when we had exerted enough downward pressure on the pole, we started the rock rolling down the hill. There was nothing that was going to stop it. It rolled off the larger trees and crushed the smaller ones. It made it all the way to the bottom of the hill, and we were whooping all the time it was on its descent.

That year we never found the perfect tree, but we had a blast looking for one. We later found the perfect cedar tree, dug it up, and planted it in the yard. From then on we decorated it outside where it was growing, and thus ended our quest to find the perfect tree.

The fun began in decorating the tree. The first order of business was popping corn and, with needle and thread, stringing it into a long rope which we wrapped around the tree. It was then decorated with ornaments which were usually second hand silver tinsel strips and decorations given to us by our teachers after removing them from the trees in the classrooms at the holiday break. It helped to have teachers who attended church services where Daddy preached. One year we came up with a string of bubbly lights, and this was the ultimate for us as we finally had electricity to be able to use them.

Daddy said that there was a 1 in 365 chance that Christ was born on December 25th, but he seriously doubted that it was in mid-winter. He maintained that it was set on that date to compete with a pagan holiday, and he did not consider Christmas Day to be more than any other day, so it was never celebrated in our family as it was with the majority of others. Nevertheless, he said that it was appropriate to remember Christ's birth, but he never put much stock in doing all the plays and manger scenes prevalent during the Christmas holidays.

Boys will be boys, and there is one stunt that we pulled a year or two at Christmastime that we thought to be fun. We would wrap a small box in Christmas paper with ribbon and take it to a bridge on the main road. We would tie a strong string to the box and throw it into the road as though it had dropped from a car. While we waited under the bridge, a passing car would many times see it and start to stop, at which time we would pull the string, grab the box, and run down the creek out of sight. When the driver would back up to retrieve the box, we would be long gone with it. I relate this as I may have given the impression that I was the perfect boy while growing up, but I want to admit that I at times did things that Mom and Dad would disapprove of.

After writing this, it occurred to me that I may have just hit on the cause that Santa never came to see me with more gifts. When he checked his list to see who had been a naughty boy, there it was: my name at the top of the list. I wish I had figured this out before I pulled those packages out of the road; maybe Santa would have been more generous toward me. Sometimes it takes age and maturity to figure things like that out, and then it is too late.

Now

Christmas is all about shopping and giving and receiving now. Somewhere between my first Christmas and now the wheels have completely come off the wagon pulling Christ's birthday cake. Merchants judge the yearly successes of their businesses by the volume of sales during Christmastime. Now many shoppers barely have time to clean up from their Thanksgiving meal before they rush to empty their wallets and max out their cards spending in anticipation of Christmas. It is not called Black Friday for nothing; the retailers expect to get out of the red for the year.

When Christmas day comes and gifts are exchanged, there is usually someone who has been forgotten, and many of those who do receive gifts praise the giver for having given them exactly what they wanted, and the gift goes into the closet or drawer and never comes out. Kids seem to get more enjoyment out of opening gifts than with playing with them. Gift return lines are long for the next few days following Christmas. I venture to say that today there is more spent on Christmas wrapping and bags than there was for gifts when I was young.

New Years

Then

On New Year's Day we changed what few calendars Dad had picked up at the general store. We never stayed up until midnight, and New Year's Day was basically just another twenty-four hours for our family.

Now

There are parties everywhere as the clock runs down, and the reverie is in full swing. As my eightieth birthday approaches, it is really no big thing, just another new calendar to hang up, which in itself is becoming a burden. Getting a good night's sleep is a better choice to welcome in the New Year.

Valentine's Day

Then

The exchange of valentines was a big thing. It was customary that every-one in the class, especially in grade school, receive one. Fortunately we had an aunt who taught school in Anniston and knew what a big thing it was to give valentines. She would normally send us enough valentines so that we were able to exchange them. They were small, sometimes punch out types that were sold by the packaged container and had different Valentine messages printed on them. Dad never bought us valentines.

Now

Don't dare to miss giving a card, flowers, and a box of candy (even though your valentine is on a strict diet). A failure to do this will be reason for a stay in the dog house. The expensive card is opened, com-plimented, and then discarded (it's the thought that counts), the flowers soon wilt, and they too find the trash can (remember, it's the thought that counts), and the candy puts on an extra pound or two.

Easter

Then

This was one time of the year that my sisters looked forward to, but not so much so us boys. We did get to wear good clean clothes on Easter Sunday, but our sisters always got new dresses which Mother would order from the Sears and Roebuck catalog. Can you imagine the excitement of two poor young girls who got to pick out an article of clothing from the Sears and Roebuck catalog to wear on Easter Day? Easter Day was a time when all females would dress up. Most young girls would have new Easter hats, ribbons in their hair, and new shoes on their feet with frilly socks. Many men in our class range just wore their best and attempted to look half-way presentable, although some of the upper echelon males sported new suits, shirts, ties and shoes, and perhaps new underwear, but that was one of the unknowns. As for us boys in the family, we did a lot of dreaming while using the toilet and looking at the catalog, but never once do I recall having the opportunity to order anything from it. There was no animosity shown toward the girls who were able to get a yearly dress from Sears, because we wanted to be proud of the way our sisters looked at Easter time.

Now

It is hard to differentiate between the qualities and styles of clothing worn on any given occasion now as there is such diversity in clothing that is being worn. Dresses are kept in the closet, and the latest fad is what will be worn. Small girls may be the exception with some families as there are still some Mothers who want to dress up their children to look their best for Easter Sunday.

Independence Day

Then

After reaching teenage years, the Fourth of July was one time of the year when a group of us boys would get a little mischievous. Some of the more prosperous ones would get fireworks, and we would make some noise. We always had cherry bombs, which were probably illegal, and we threw many of them where it would be disturbing. We never used them in a destructive way such as putting them in mailboxes, but we thought it to be fun to throw one near where a group had gathered. There was a nearby fire tower that we would climb and throw firecrackers and cherry bombs from the top where they would echo throughout the neighborhood.

My friend whose father owned the coal mine would always sneak four or five sticks of dynamite from the powder house and blow them up after darkness fell. This was done in a large, vacant pasture near his house. This shook the neighborhood and served as the loudest firecracker around. This is proof positive that we were still on the climb up Fool's Hill when we pulled stunts like this as it was nothing short of a miracle that we didn't get blown off the hill. Our Guardian Angel was working overtime at times such as this.

Halloween

Then

We were never any part of turning over toilets, throwing eggs or water balloons, jacking up cars, and putting the rear axles on blocks so that the tires would spin after the car was cranked and put in gear causing them to go nowhere. Later kids put VW Rabbits on low lying buildings. We would dress up in Halloween outfits and go out to the main road and make a weak attempt to scare people who drove by. We never did any trick-or-treating, because there were no people in our community who had any treats, and we were not permitted to do any tricks. If there were those who did have treats they would be either fruit or popcorn balls. There was no hope of getting any candy.

Now

Creatures of all descriptions are out on Halloween night carrying bags and buckets, and in one night a kid will get more candy than I ever had in a young lifetime. Over the years, there have been changes as there was a time when kids would go to every house they could reach in a night ringing doorbells and shouting, "Trick or treat!" Now many families use a safer method of trick-or-treating by having safe specified areas at businesses or churches where there will be trunk-or-treat parties. Parents will allow their children still to ring doorbells in trick-or-treating but only in safe neighborhoods where the residents are known. At one time, it was not safe to drive around on Halloween night as there would be those who would pepper passing cars with eggs, water balloons, missiles, or other objects, some destructive, but there seems to have been an effort on the part of law enforcement to reduce these types of activities on Halloween. It remains a good time of the year for makers of toilet paper, as there are some yards that will have enough toilet paper wrapped around trees and bushes to provide wipes for a year or more.

Thanksgiving

Then

My sister remembers Thanksgiving as being the time of the year that our maternal Grandmother would visit us from Anniston where she lived with and kept house for another of her daughters. Our Grandmother would, in the early years, catch a train and get off at the Big Ridge whistle stop which was located near the place we caught the school bus each day. She never learned to drive as was customary for women at that time, and in later years she rode a bus to visit us or her son-in-law would transport her to our house.

Thanksgiving was also the time of the year that Dad considered to be hog killing time, as the weather was getting cold enough that the meat would not spoil before he could get it salted and in the smoke house to preserve it for the months ahead. Hog killing was usually a community affair when neighbors would come over to help with the butchering, and in turn they would take home a portion of the meat. There was always sausage to be ground and lard to be extracted from the fat. Mother would trim the fat from the meat and place it in an iron wash tub and cook until the lard was rendered out leaving the pork cracklings, which we kids always gobbled up. We ate high off the hog on Thanksgiving as we had that fresh meat to enjoy. We always kept two or three hogs which supplied pork that kept our smokehouse well stocked.

On Thanksgiving, we also had chicken to eat. One of us boys would catch the big rooster we had fattened up for Thanksgiving, give it to Mother who would wring its neck, and then dress it for the Thanksgiving meal. We never raised turkeys, and Dad would certainly not buy one when we had roosters. There would always be brown gravy and cornbread dressing. Sweet potatoes were always on the menu as well as vegetables which had been canned during the summer. Sometimes Dad would get some bananas and vanilla wafers, and Mother would make a banana pudding for dessert.

Now

It's a bad time of the year for turkeys.

CHAPTER TWENTY-FOUR

PRICES

Then

Let's have some fun with this topic; otherwise, you may have read this far and then I throw this subject in and ruin everything. When I go back to the year of my birth, 1938, and do a little comparison between now and then, I am afraid that I will be unable to paint a rosy picture of the differences. There is a plus as we consider this, and that is that the quality of products and the quality of life have made great improvements. In almost every aspect of life, we are much better off now than in 1938. Houses are better, cars are better, roads are better, the amount and quality of food is better, there are more comforts and conveniences today, but this has not come without a price. There are many aspects which could be compared then as to now, but for the sake of brevity I will concentrate on income, wages, buying power of the dollar and the price of food items only. The prices of all goods and chattels could not be reasonably compared in this writing. Even the extent that I will explore this issue may be of little interest to some, but there has been such a change in the prices of things during my lifetime that I feel compelled to write about them. I will make a disclaimer here and confess that almost all that I have written about the price of things when I was young comes straight from my memory. I do remember some prices from the days that I helped out doing stocking and delivering groceries in the small country store located near our house, but I could not possibly know prices from the year of my birth, so this section will be largely from research from then and a comparison to today. To do this I will compare the *Then* and the *Now* simultaneously.

We will begin with a comparison of the price of selected objects. In the first line, we list the actual cost the goods sold for in 1938. In the second line, we compare the 1938 price to what the items would cost today with dollar values in 1938 money. The third line shows the actual cost today after inflation. The first two prices will be listed as the USD (United States Dollar) defined price and the third as Actual Price. I will be using data from 2013 which is four years removed from the date of this writing, but will show how the changing times have affected our buying power. In the not too distant future I suspect that there will be those who will look at this writing and make comparisons to what we have now and what they have then. Time moves on!

According to the Bureau of Labor Statistics $100 dollars in 1938 money is now calculated to be the equivalent of $1,784.33 (2018 or 80 years later). There has been an inflation rate of 3.67% per year or 1684.3% higher than prices in 1938. A post from *mybudget360* illustrates the difference.

Then: *Now:*

Item	USD Price 1938	USD Price 2013	Actual Price 2013
New house	$3,900.00	$64,599.83	$245,800.00
New car	$860.00	$14,244.55	$31,250.00
Average rent	$27.00/Mo.	$447.22/Mo.	$821.00/Mo.
Harvard tuition	$420.00 /Yr.	$6,956.69 /Yr.	$54,496.00/ Yr.
Movie ticket	25 cents	$4.14	$7.84
Gasoline	10 cents/ gal	$1.66/ gal	$3.24/ gal.
U.S. postage stamp	3 cents	50 cents	46 (49/ 2017)
Average income	$1,731.00/Yr.	$28,671.00/Yr.	$27,000.00/Yr.

The Mint Act of 1791 established an index of the purchasing power of the U.S. Dollar. It began at 100% and was based on the standard. In 1971, the last link between U.S. currency and gold was cut. From the time of the establishment of the index and 2004, the U.S. Dollar lost 92% of its purchasing power.

The year that I was born, 1938, the grocery bill was not as costly as today, especially in the country where people grew a substantial amount of the food that they ate. There were staples such as flour and sugar which were purchased at small local grocery stores. Nevertheless, prices were low, but so were wages. After some research, I am able to submit a price list that compares grocery prices from 1938, then food prices the year I became a teenager twelve years later (I obviously don't remember the 1938 prices but do recall some as a teenager thus I add the 1951 prices to this list), and then actual prices in Oct. 2017. As it seems that the Walmart Super Center is the favorite place to buy groceries in this area, the current prices as shown were the ones listed on the shelves and copied by this writer. Whenever possible, the lowest listed price was the one used in this search. Some items such as milk (which normally sells for $3.29) and eggs were on sale because of local competition, and the sale price as listed on the date of my visit is the one shown. Merchandising has made a drastic change during the years since 1938, and many items can now be bought at various prices dependent upon brand and quantity. An attempt was made to find the lowest or comparable price as compared to the 1938 price. Again, a post from *The Peoples History* clearly reveals the differences.

Item	1938 Price	1951 Price	Oct. 2017 Price
Loaf of sliced bread	5 Cents	12 Cents	$1.58
Eggs	18 Cents/doz.	49 cents/doz.	78 Cents/doz.
Bran Flakes, box	10 Cents		$3.21
Bananas	19 Cents/lb.	29 Cents/lb.	59 Cents/lb.
Peanut Butter	23 Cents/Qt.		$3.32/28 Oz
Toilet Tissue	9 Cents/2 rolls	5 cents roll	$3.36/3 rolls
Tooth Paste	27 Cents	29 Cents	$2.96
Bacon sliced.	38 Cents/ lb.	35 Cents/lb.	$4.38/lb.
Ketchup	9 Cents		$1.92/13.5 oz.
Iceberg lettuce	7 Cents/head		$1.64/head
Potatoes	18 Cents/10 lb.	35 Cents/10lb.	$4.94/10/lb
Sugar	$1.25/25 lb bag	43cents/5 lb.	$1.89/5 lb.
Chuck Roast	15 Cents/lb.	59 Cents/lb.	$4.46/lb.
Chicken	20 Cents/lb.	43 Cents/lb.	Varied as cut
Best Steak	22 Cents/lb.	59 Cents/lb.	$9.97/lb.
Campbell Tomato Soup	25Cents/4 cans	10Cents/can	$1.58/can
Oranges	25 Cents/2 doz.	69 Cents/2 doz.	$4.98/3 lbs.
Vitamin D. Milk	50 Cents/gal.		$1.78/gal.
Coffee	39 Cents/lb.	37 Cents/lb.	$6.38/24oz
Hamburger Meat		89 Cents/3 lbs.	$3.72/lb.
Margarine		19 Cents/ lb.	97 Cents/lb.

As I do very little grocery shopping, when I was in Walmart comparing prices I was struck by the difference in merchandising today compared to when I worked in our local country store. Then, the local wholesale salesman would make weekly visits to see what stock was running low and send a truck to replenish what was needed. If a customer wanted a specific item that was not in stock, the grocer would make a note and have it delivered when the truck ran again. This was because of limited shelf space. Now, store shelves are fully stocked with anything imaginable that one would want to buy. I also noticed that one can pay almost any price for the same food item depending upon the brand name and quantity purchased. The store brand normally costs less, but if one prefers a certain brand name, that will be stocked also. This made it more difficult to get an accurate comparable price when I was working on the above list.

The amount of shelf space devoted to one food type was also interesting to me. Cereal of all brands, grains, coatings, and fruit mixture occupy one whole long row of shelving. I am convinced that cereal products occupied more shelving in Wal-Mart than the entire store had where Dad bought his groceries.

Another difference in today's grocery shopping is the use of discount coupons. There are many shoppers who are faithful users of coupons cut from sale ads, magazines, and newspapers, as well as electronically produced coupons. In the past there have been different gimmicks designed to lure shoppers such as S&H Green Stamps which were the most popular, but they had competitors such as Gold Bond and Blue Chip Stamps. At one time Sperry & Hutchinson who issued S&H Green Stamps claimed that they distributed three times as many stamps as did the U.S. Post Office, and that their rewards catalog was the largest publication in the United States. Based on the amount of the purchase, stamps were handed out at the cash register, and when certain quantities of stamps had been accumulated they could be traded for items available within that amount. Available rewards could be ordered from their catalog or redeemed at redemption centers located in most major cities. From the time I was born until the mid-eighties, the stamps were popular, but with the depression in the eighties, discounted groceries in lieu of giving stamps eased the stamps out of favor with merchants and consumers. Some local grocery retailers provide a box where numbered coupons are handed out according to the amount spent, and a weekly drawing will reward the holder of that number with a certain amount of money. Another angle on this is to have one sign his or her name and give a telephone number on the back of the cash register receipt, place it in the box provided for that purpose, and if that receipt is drawn at the given time, you will be reimbursed for the amount spent as recorded on that receipt.

As far as I can remember I never once went shopping for food until I left home after graduating from high school. When money was available to me, I would go to the store and buy a soda pop and a piece of candy (Zero, Payday, Baby Ruth, and Three Musketeers were my favorites) or Moon Pies. For these items I was a very thrifty shopper. Coca Cola came in refillable glass bottles which were smaller than most other drinks, so buying a Coke was out of the question. I never cared for 7-Up, so that narrowed the choice down a bit. Nehi was a good choice as were Pepsis and Royal Crown (RC) Cola. A local family, The Craven's in Parrish, bottled Try Me, and had a good selection of fruit flavors and cola, and was also a good buy. All soft drinks were sold in returnable glass bottles that required a deposit that was reimbursed upon return. My first recollection was that they sold for a nickel with about a penny extra required for the deposit if taken from the store. Most of the time I would drink my beverage while at the store in order to save my penny. In fact, after a period of time all drinks but Try Me went up to 6 cents plus the deposit, so I switched totally to Try Me to avoid the inflation. Today when I pay a dollar for the same size bottle and think that I got a bargain, I think of the good old days. At least today I don't have to pay a deposit on the bottle (in Alabama).

CHAPTER TWENTY-FIVE

RATIONING

Then

During the first few years of my life the Second World War was raging, and many items were rationed because of the war effort. I can still remember some of those days because of the difficulty the war caused to almost every family. Food rationing started in the spring of 1942, and all rationing ended in 1946 when I was eight years old. I was at the age that I can clearly remember when Dad, and later Mom after Dad left to join the war effort, had to use rationing stamps in order to buy some foods. At the beginning of the war, Dad was preaching for a congregation in Fayette, Alabama, but after he left to guard munitions at the Anniston Ordinance Depot, we moved back to Mom's old home place where she could make a garden to help feed us hungry kids. As store bought food was scarce or even unavailable, it was incumbent upon Mother to see that we were properly fed. The times were not only hard on us, but many other families also struggled until the war was won, the surviving men returned to their families, and food rationing was ended.

Tires were the first item to be rationed. In December of 1941, because of the shortage of rubber which was necessary for the war effort, the owners of automobiles could possess no more than five tires. Any additional tires were taken by the government. In order to get additional tires, there had to be given proof of need. Tires at that time were frequently worn until holes developed in them. When this happened, a "boot" was placed over the hole and the tire continued to be used. There were no tubeless tires at that time, and an inserted tube made it possible to continue using the tire. Do I remember when this was taking place? You betcha! Who could forget the rough ride created by booted tires? There was no way that the tire could be balanced with a boot in it, and as the car traveled there was often shimming and bumps when the booted part of the tire rotated over the road. Fortunately, the government had set the speed limit at thirty-five miles per hour in order to conserve gasoline and tire wear. I remember one day while standing in our yard in Fayette, a large truck passed with about three rear axles and Dad commenting about the number of tires that were required on the truck. Everything it seemed was centered on doing what was necessary to win the war.

Gasoline was next to be rationed. To receive a gasoline rationing card, the owner had to prove ownership of a car and prove a need for it. There were numbers shown on the gasoline card which designated the amount of gasoline that could be purchased. They were as follows:

A—3 to 4 gallons a week.

B—for defense workers—8 gallons a week

C—persons essential to war effort such as doctor—as needed

T—trucker

X—unlimited supply, Ministers of Religion, Firemen, Civil Defense workers

As Dad was a minister of religion, he had no problem getting gasoline; paying for it was the problem. A good bit of the time he was secluded while guarding the munitions and had no need for gasoline.

Following this, a number of items appeared on the rationing list. Automobiles were next being rationed during the first of 1942. They were cut from production, and the automobile companies switched to the production of trucks, tanks, and other war material. Any automobile left in the inventory could only be sold to doctors and clergy. The automobile factories had stopped making cars by February 1942. In March, typewriters were no longer manufactured, bicycles in May, and following that a number of things came under rationing. Tobacco supplies and liquor were diverted from the civilian market, private ownership of radio transmitters was forbidden for security reasons, paper could be used only for essential purposes, book size shrunk with no extra pages and only paperbacks. Magazine and newspaper size were slightly smaller and ad size limited. Textile production was diverted to military needs, and cloth, thread, and yarns were less accessible. Silk was needed for parachutes and medical supplies, so silk stockings and clothing were no longer obtainable. Wool was needed for the war effort to provide troops fighting in winter weather such as the conditions in the Battle of the Bulge. Rubber belts, auto parts, and lubricants soon made the list of rationed goods. Auto racing, including the Indy 500, was forbidden because of the rubber and gasoline shortage.

Sugar was the first commodity to be rationed. Some 5,500 local rationing boards made up mostly of volunteers were selected by local officials, and they were placed in charge of issuing the cards and stamps needed to purchase the rationed goods. Every American was issued a ration book that had removable stamps. After the stamps were used up for the month, no more food of any type could be bought. On May 4, 1942, sugar could be purchased only by using a stamp. The limit was ½ lb. per person per week. Bakeries, ice cream factories, and commercial users were cut to 70% of what they used before rationing. There were supplemented allowances of sugar for home canning, canning jellies, jams, fruit, and butter/preserves, but there was a requirement that the household members who were authorized to consume them be identified.

Coffee was rationed in November and a person was limited to 1 lb. every five weeks. Meats, lard, shortening, cooking oil, cheese, butter, margarine, processed foods (canned and frozen), dried fruit, canned milk, firewood, jellies, fruit butter, and other commodities were also rationed. Dog food could not be sold in tin cans and dehydrated dog food was used. The shortage of metal was so severe that by April 1st toothpaste that was being sold in metal containers had to be sold only when the old container was turned in. One person reported seeing a long line of people waiting to get ½ pound of lard which was being scooped from a large barrel.

Where did our family fit in all this? As I drain my memory bank of this era, I think that I recall that we got stamps for all of us, but as I remember, not all of them were used each month. Because of the lack of funding and our sparse existence, only the ones of essentials were used. The lack of money restricted our purchase power.

Now

SHOP TILL YOU DROP (or run out of money and max your cards)!

CHAPTER TWENTY-SIX

INTEGRITY

Then

This topic was suggested by an individual who had been shortchanged by a group of workers at his new house. He needed to have it underpinned with brick, and he hired it to be done. Before they had finished he had to be away from his house for a period of time, and he went ahead and paid them for the agreed upon price for the completion of the job. When he returned the workers were gone and had not laid another brick after he left. He never saw them again.

I will make this topic brief as there is not a whole lot to be discussed that is not already known. We all have been victims of dishonest dealings at one time or another and are vigilant when dealing with others to insure an honest result.

There have always been deadbeats and always will be. It seems, however, that there are more of them today than there were those in times past. As far as I am aware, my father never signed a written contract to either do a job or to have one done. An agreed upon amount and a handshake were as good as a signed contract, and all non-agreed upon issues were solved to the satisfaction of both parties. It was an honorable thing to say of a person that they were as good as their word.

If something was borrowed, it was returned after use, generally speaking. If a cook wanted to borrow something like flour or sugar, the amount was returned after the borrower had replenished their supply.

If a neighbor needed a tool that they did not have, it was loaned if it was not in use, with the assurance of knowing that it would be returned when the job was finished. If there was damage done to the item, it would be repaired to the original condition in which it was borrowed. The exchange went both ways, and it was a practice that neighbor help neighbor.

Most business owners operated upon a credit system and prospered in doing so. Credit was established at one's favorite business and purchases were made throughout the week or month, and payment was made after payday. Of course, there were those to whom credit would not be extended because of their reputation, and there were others who failed to pay their debts, but by and large people were to be trusted. It did not take long for word to get around if a person was not to be trusted, and then most required that person to have money in hand when a purchase was made.

Now

In most business transactions today, it is prudent to have a signed contract whether buying or selling. In this contract it is also wise to make sure that specifics are included. It is also not wise to pay upfront before the agreed upon results are finished and satisfactory.

I assume that there may be some out there, but I personally know of no business owner who does regular credit business today. Personal checks are not accepted in more and more places because of those that are passed without sufficient funds in the bank to cover them. Personal identification is required in places that still accept checks and also in check card transactions. There are so many scams and dishonest dealings on phones that many are hesitant to answer them now, figuring that they could get caught up unknowingly in a scam and be unaware of it. It has reached the point to where if persons are unknown to you, be leery of them.

Even many marriages today will not be performed before a pre-nuptial agreement has been reached and signed. It seems obvious that even marrying partners don't trust one another in the modern era. This, I learned recently, not only covers financial and domestic matters, but the number of times per week or month that sexual activities are required.

I promised at the beginning of this topic that I would make it brief. I am a man of my word.

CHAPTER TWENTY-SEVEN

MANNERS

Then

"Mind your manners," was a quote that I often heard from my parents when we would go to visit or eat with a family. It was important that we were on our best behavior when we were in public. "Always remember the Golden Rule," was another admonition that we would hear. We were taught to be considerate of others and to be courteous in all that we did.

At a very early age, I was taught to always say "please" and "thank you" and to say "I'm sorry" when I accidently ran into someone or made another blunder. Women were to be addressed as "ma'am" and men as "sir." Affirmative answers were to be "yes ma'am" or "yes, sir" and negative answers "no ma'am" or "no, sir". An affirmative or negative head shake was not a proper response. To never interrupt a person who was speaking was also taught.

We were taught to always be thankful for what we had. At meal time all family members sat, and nothing was touched before the blessing was said. Every boy took turns saying the blessing with heads bowed and eyes closed until the prayer ended. After the blessing was said, the food was passed around the table, always going in a counter-clockwise direction. "Don't heap your plate," was another manner that was taught as the food was passed. If there was any food left on the serving platters, extra helpings were then permitted, but only after everyone had a chance to get a serving. "Don't eat too fast, chew your food," would be the forthcoming command if Mother thought that a child was eating their food too fast. Mother always prepared enough food to allow every family member to have their fair share, and hopefully enough to feed the hungry dogs as they were fed only table scraps.

When we had guests for dinner or were guests at other homes, we were taught to always let the adults get their food first. This allowed them to get the first pick of chicken parts or other meats. After they got what they wanted, the kids got what was left. If we left during or after the meal while others were still seated, we were taught to ask, "May I be excused?" before leaving. When guests were present, we were not to put our elbows on the table, but with no guest present, this infraction was largely ignored.

One thing that Mother insisted upon was that while eating in the school lunch room, after we had finished eating we were to tell the cooks, "I enjoyed my lunch!" This I did after every meal, and I knew of no other kids, with the exception of those in our family, which did that. The cooks always seemed appreciative of this gesture. I can truthfully say that we were sincere when we told them this as there was no food which I balked at eating, although spinach was not high on my preferred list.

"Ladies first," was another courtesy that was instilled in us as we interacted with a mixed gender group. We were taught to open doors and hold them open until all had entered. Being polite with a smile as we met others was encouraged. We were taught how to handshake properly and how to greet others in a mannerly way. Excessive talking and questions were discouraged, and listening to what others had to say was the proper way to communicate with others.

Basic table manners were expected, but we were never big on that which was considered to be the appropriate placement and use of tableware. Mostly, all we were expected to do was to eat with a fork and not a spoon unless a spoon was required, and not to talk with food in our mouths. Normally, unless a liquid was served, only a fork was used in the place setting, as all dirty dishes and utensils had to be washed in water that had to be drawn from the well, and Mother tried to eliminate the excessive use of plates, glassware, and utensils.

For our daily meals we never had fancy tableware. In fact, Mother believed in using the basics to eat from. Therefore, she bought cake pans for each of us kids to use as plates. Inside the pan she placed our initials so that we got the same pan to eat from at each meal. I still have my pan with W's scratched in all four directions, which served as my plate as I grew up. Practicality took precedence over formality in our everyday meals.

Now

It might very well be that I am just a cranky old man, but I sometimes cringe when I see the lack of manners that are displayed by the younger generation. On the other hand, I also sometimes notice when young people are courteous, and it is obvious that they have been taught to use good manners. I will emphasize that no one should give up on this generation of our newest citizens, as I have observed too many positive things that encourage me to believe that we will leave our country in good hands; that we are going to be alright when they become of age to be the leaders of their generation. When disaster strikes, many are on the front lines in providing assistance. I smile when I read of teenagers and young adults who use their school break to volunteer to help to make conditions better for the disadvantaged.

Just today as my wife was preparing to enter a local store the door opened as a family consisting of parents and a very young son were leaving. While making their exit the mother said to the boy, "Be a gentleman and hold the door open for the lady." The mother then turned to my wife and commented, "He needs to learn how to be a gentleman." Smiling, my wife said, "Good ideal." It is encouraging to know that civility is still alive!

Having given credit where credit is due, I also observe some young people who could not tell you the definition of the word courtesy, and this group seems to be gaining majority status. It now seems that many had rather greet you with a middle finger as opposed to a smile. Be careful at an open door because you could be knocked down when they rush to enter first. One of the big differences between the time I was taught manners and what I see today is the use of foul language. No curse or foul words seem to be off limits now. Words that would get a kid's mouth washed out with soap then are standard vocabulary now. When I observe this, which is far too often, I wonder where parents are in regard to this behavior and why they have allowed such conduct. I can only praise my parents for the guidance which they gave me in my formative years and condemn any parent who would bring a child into this world and then fail to provide proper supervision as they mature. Of equal interest to me is that girls are just as likely to greet you with a finger and then rain a shower of foul words on you as do the boys. When I was young, I knew some males who had a vocabulary of curse words but no females.

If I attempted to show examples of bad manners which I now observe, I would only fail to include them all. This to me is disturbing as these are the people to whom we will entrust the future of our nation. This is conduct which I think will be detrimental in the future. As I said at the beginning of this topic, maybe I have just become cranky in my old age and fail to take into consideration that kids will be kids, but I have also lived long enough to know that in the future kids will then be adults who will benefit from learning proper manners and conduct. Most of these individuals will themselves become mothers and fathers who should be capable of giving their children the parental supervision which they need.

I believe it to be important to properly instill in a child good conduct and proper manners because these traits will be advantageous in being successful later in life. Hard, back-breaking labor seems to be the occupation that attracts the uneducated, uncouth, bad-mannered, foul-mouthed, rude individual. This is not a blanket indictment on those who do such work as there are many people of outstanding moral values who hold these jobs, but seldom would you see an impolite bad-mannered person successfully hold a job requiring frequent contact with the public. If for no other reason than to train children to successfully prepare themselves to work in jobs requiring mannerly interaction with the public, they should be taught how to conduct themselves properly while among others. The public expects to be treated politely and with respect.

CHAPTER TWENTY-EIGHT

RACE RELATIONS

I do not hesitate to wade in on this subject as I feel comfortable in doing so. In fact, I have something to say that I feel needs to be said. People must speak for themselves regarding this matter, but I feel compelled to include my feelings regarding racial matters as I complete the draining of my memory bank.

Then

I first will go back to the sixties when integration was a big topic of discussion. My father, who was a minister of the gospel, was asked what he would do if black people entered the church building where he was preaching. His reply was simple. "I would try to save their souls. All people's souls are colorless just like mine." This is the attitude that our family always had regarding mankind. My father would get into the pulpit and preach that God is no respecter of persons and those who are saved will live together for an eternity in heaven. We cannot discriminate here and expect that practice to continue if we reach Heaven. In fact, if we cannot live together in peace here on this earth and cannot accept people who are outwardly different than we are, I think it doubtful that we will be headed in an upward direction after death. Jesus commanded that his disciples were to go into all the world and preach the gospel to EVERY creature, and that includes all skin colors.

When one gets beyond the color of skin of an individual, they will realize that all under it is like everyone else. The internal organs do not carry pigmented skin, and all races function like all the other races and skin colors. It is only the outward pigment that is different. The Bible also states that mankind is of one blood. I have been diligent in donating blood to the American Red Cross not knowing who might be helped by my donation, nor does it matter. It could be of either gender or race. If they have my blood type and need blood, no matter who it might be, I am happy that I might be able to contribute to the effort to restore health. I have had the good fortune to have been able to contribute almost twenty-one gallons of blood, and somewhere those some 165 units that I have donated, I feel, have helped individuals of all races. I am pleased that there were those who carried my blood in their bodies as they healed from their illness or wounds no matter who they were or the cause of their need for blood. To help those with need for blood was my intent as I gave the blood. Additionally, if I should ever need blood I certainly would not quibble with the race or gender of the donor.

I consider it to be amusing that many who are born with white skin are not happy about it. Billions of dollars are spent yearly by those who want color in their complexion. Millions of those who are seeking to be glamorous head to the beaches or tanning parlors to get some color in their skin. It is a great virtue to realize that we were brought into this world as was determined by the race and color of those who conceived us, and we should be proud of our heritage. This is the life that has been so miraculously given us, and we should exploit it fully in a respectable way as we seek happiness and contentment. The Apostle Paul says it well as he writes his first letter to Timothy. He reminds him that, "Godliness with contentment is great gain. We brought nothing into this world, and it is certain we will carry nothing out. Having food and clothing let us be content." In his letter to the Hebrews he tells them to "be content with such things as you have." In the Sermon on the Mount when Jesus is commenting on contentment he adds, "Which of you by taking thought can add one cubic to his stature?" He is saying that we are who we are and we cannot change that. If you are short and want to be tall, or vice versa, forget it and appreciate who you are. If we are white and want to be black, a suntan will only partially take us there. If we are black and want to be white, it is too late to consult

Michael Jackson as to how to best pull that off. The bottom line in all of this is that we are blessed that we have breath in our body no matter the color of the nose that breathes the air. Anyone who would belittle any individual because of the circumstances of their birth fails to realize that they too are the products of their race. They are no better or worse than any other person no matter who they are or where they are from. Before demeaning another, one should first get on their knees and say a prayer of thanksgiving for life, and that all men everywhere, receive God's blessings.

It is now time for me to recount my memories of my relationship with blacks when I was young. My memory bank is practically void of any interaction that I had with them while in school. It is merely the fact that I was never around people of color that I have no recollection of any contact or dealings with them. We lived in a rural area where only whites lived. The black population was congregated in one section in each of the nearest towns, and I knew of no blacks who lived elsewhere. The blacks had their own school, and I am even at a loss as to where that school building was located when I was young. Perhaps they all attended school in the largest, nearest town. It was later after the threat of integration that new school buildings were built in the two neighboring towns for the black students, perhaps as an attempt to avoid the inevitable. They were used only a very short time before the black students were transferred to the larger schools when integration was ordered. Both buildings then sat unoccupied until the high school building in one town burned, and the vacated school that was built for black students was enlarged and remodeled and then occupied by all students; the other school building that housed black students in the other town was sold to a religious group. I went about my business of growing up, and the thought never occurred to me that there were black children doing the same thing. As my school years were long before integration, the plight of those unseen citizens living in another section of town never appeared on my radar screen. They were out of sight and out of mind with nothing to call attention to their presence. I never went into the black section of town as it was out of the way on my trips to and from home. They had their own churches, and I never knew of them attempting to worship with the white population.

Now I will get into the nitty-gritty of what little I know about the relationship that other whites besides myself had with the blacks, or colored people as they were usually called. While I worked at the five and dime store, I never observed any disrespectful conduct displayed to shoppers of any race. The owners of the store had many faithful black customers, and there seemed to always be friendship between them. As far as I can remember, a black shopper was just as likely to be extended credit as the white. The blacks, in fact, seemed to be more courteous than many of the white shoppers. They would normally address a man with a "sir" attached to the answer and a woman as "ma'am". It was part of their vocabulary to say 'yessir' or 'nosir' or 'yesma'am' or 'noma'am', as if they were each one word. I remember that they would usually say it with emphasis. That is a far cry from the 'yea' that was a common answer that was often forthcoming from the white population.

I could not leave this subject without addressing the N----- word, and it was commonly used back then. I grew up with people referring to the black population as Blacks, Colored People, Negroes, or N------ (which I will now refer to as the N word). As best that I can remember, the first three name designations were the most common in usage, but there were times that the N word was used. At that time, I never considered it to be a slam on the black population, but most of the time it was used as a way to describe a person or place. Let me explain. If one asked where a black person lived, the answer might be "over in the N quarters by the train depot." This response could come from either a white or black as this was a common designation for the area, and no one, as far as I could tell, took offense by the usage. It would not be uncommon for someone to say about a black person, "He is a good N, and you can trust him with everything that you have." That certainly would not be spoken in a disrespectful way, nor would it be used to generalize the population as a whole. Granted, there were some who used the word more often than others, and I could not say that it was not used in offensive ways by some, but this was never the case with a lot of people who grew up hearing the word used and did not use it in a demeaning way. I can truthfully say that my family, including myself, felt no animosity toward anyone of any race or color. We are all God's creatures.

Now

Forgive me and my simplicities, but it is hard for me to grasp how racism continues to be such a major issue. A black President has been elected for two terms, and there are equal opportunities for advancement to anyone no matter the race. Those who think that the world owes them a living and expect everything to be handed to them will live in a state of disillusionment and can never be satisfied, because they will always expect more. These people will never be happy with the status-quo. They perceive that almost all actions are discriminatory (this includes whites and blacks) in nature, and therefore they claim racism.

But it is not just the lower class that keeps the idea of rampant racism alive. It is my observation that this has become a tool for elected officials and highly ranked individuals to exploit their causes. If things do not go exactly their way, they cry "racism." No matter that the outgoing president was black and there are many cities with black mayors and other elected officials, competent people of color in high cabinet and governmental positions, along with sports athletes and entertainers who make enormous paychecks. After sixty years of integration reforms, one begins to wonder where this will all end and just what it will take to satisfy some people without giving them the country and supporting their every cause.

If we could look eighty years into the future, it would be interesting to know just how this racial conflict has played out, if it has even been resolved. If the past sixty-five years are any example, it may still be an issue with some into the distant future. One thing is almost certain. White couples will still have children that are born white and blacks the same. I do not foresee that there will be genetic engineering that has reached the point where a child can be born with the exact skin color the parent desires, but it would not be surprising that there are now those in the labs across the nation who are working to make it happen, just as there are in gender identification. At this writing, there is a big movement in transgender activities, and if one who happened to be born a different gender than what they had wished, no matter that parents had messed up at time of conception and allowed the wrong sperm to reach that egg first, not to worry: a gender change will take care of that little problem. Now both bathrooms will be accessible so the gender signs at the entrance can just be ignored, or even eliminated, and entrance can be made at the most convenient one, or maybe there might even be just one for all. I am mentioning this as who knows just where this genetic engineering will lead. Will all new babies be born with nice suntan colored pigments or whatever may be ordered? The suntan parlor industry and beachfront properties may help to slow this down as it would be harmful for their businesses. Will cloning be an acceptable practice with humans? There are a lot of questions which only the eighty years can answer.

CHAPTER TWENTY-NINE

SWEEPING OUT

As I wrote this, there were many events that came to my mind which I felt were not of significant value to hang on to. I will say that I did not leave any dirty linen in the closet that I did not want to reveal. As with every person, there were mistakes which I made along the way and some things that were embarrassing, but if one gets out of the house among the public these things will inevitably happen. It is not healthful to dwell on the negatives in life which all will have, but we should be pleased with the positives. You are who you are, that special person who has been waiting from the beginning of mankind for your time to enjoy Gods creation, and I admonish you not to blow it. It is life that has been given you to do with it as you please. There is a guide book which was given by the Creator to lead you through the obstacles that will daily confront you. This guidebook warns of an adversary who delights in derailing individuals so as to get them on his side. Things that people should avoid so as to enhance their lives are written as cautions in this book, as are the things that will make for a happier and fuller life. Even though a person may not be religious and considers that heaven and hell are a myth and therefore would not read the book in order to be saved or lost after death, it would still be beneficial to know what will enrich lives and what will destroy them. As a probation and parole officer for over thirty years, my job would have been a lot less complicated had the thousands of those who had been convicted of crimes with whom I counseled only read that guide and followed it. Additionally, as I think of the huge expenses that are required to finance our federal, state, and local law enforcements, jails, prisons, rehab efforts, injuries, accidental loss of life due to substance abuse, military expenses, thefts of properties, homicides, broken homes and families, vandalism, neglected children, promiscuity, pornography, sexual abuse, pedophiles, con artists and scammers—where and when will all this end?

The answer to the above is that it will not end. These things have been happening since the beginning of time and will continue until time ends. Only a few will read the guidebook that the Creator has left with us, and even fewer will follow that guide. Therefore it is not my intention to preach a sermon here as I can do no better than make the recommendation here that one follow the path that is outlined in that book, the Bible. If faithfully followed, I can assure you that your life will be enriched. One may not believe that there is an eternal heaven and therefore not be interested in getting there, but that person still has a lifetime on this earth and following the Biblical guide would still be a wise thing to do.

God only knows how many days, weeks, months, or years I have left on earth before I explore the hereafter. What I do know is that I must use the remaining time I have allotted to do all that I can to help make the world a little better when I leave than when I got here. Obviously, as a single individual, I cannot solve every problem or help every needed individual. I can only do my part and make an effort to shed a light and be an example to those who are living in a world of darkness and who, sadly, waste the precious lifetime which they were given. In this effort, I can be certain that I will have the backing and support of Him who has blessed me and has given me life and left the guide that I have followed while ascending and descending Fool's Hill, traveled down Memory Lane, and crossed eighty years of time.

About the Author

Wheeler Pounds grew up in rural Alabama, and he has always possessed a deep connection to the outdoors and his Native American heritage. He is a member of the Echota Cherokee Tribe of Alabama, of which he is the chief of the Blue Clan. For thirty years he was employed by the State Board of Pardons and Paroles and was an adjunct instructor of Criminal Justice at Faulkner University.

Since retiring, he has been able to devote time to his favorite hobby of being an avid hiker. He has backpacked the majority of the National Parks in the United States but maintains that his favorite is Bankhead National Forest, which is near his home. He is also a committed husband, father, and grandfather and has dedicated a significant portion of his life to volunteer work.

Wheeler resides in Walker County, Alabama with his wife, Judi, where he spends time with family and friends and continues to foster his passion for nature.

Thanks for reading *Up Fool's Hill Down Memory Lane Across Time*!

Wheeler would greatly appreciate feedback for his work to be left on Amazon, Goodreads, or any other of your favorite review platforms.

Also by Wheeler Pounds: *Secrets of the Cherokee Hideaway* Series

The Cherokee Hideaway
ISBN: 978-1934610640

The Cellar Vault
ISBN: 978-1934610794

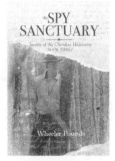

The Spy Sanctuary
ISBN: 978-1934610244

If you enjoyed this book, try these other titles from
Bluewater Publications

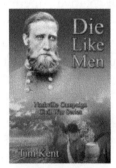

Die Like Men
Tim Kent
ISBN: 978-1934610626

The Secret of Wattensaw Bayou
M.E. Hubbs
ISBN: 978-1934610763

Betrayed
Tim Kent
ISBN: 978-1934610817

Never Smile Again
Tim Kent
ISBN: 978-1934610688

CPSIA information can be obtained
at www.ICGtesting.com
Printed in the USA
BVHW031300020419
544369BV00003B/3/P

9 781934 610152